THE HUM...
Er...
Bo...

GW00568485

Humo...

1927–1996

PLACE OF BIRTH:

Dayton, Ohio

GIVEN NAME:

Erma Louise Fiste Harris

BIRTHDAY:

February 21

SIGN:

Pisces

BLONDE MOMENT:

selling her first column for three dollars

CROWNING ACHIEVEMENT:

America's leading female humorist

BLONDO-BIOGRAPHY:

twelve collections of her columns, including *The Grass Is Always Greener over the Septic Tank*

WEB SITE:

www.ermamuseum.org

Erma Bombeck owes her unique brand of self-deprecating humor to her Midwestern beginnings. Born into a working-class family, her sixteen-year-old mother worked at the local factory, and her father was a crane operator.

Erma published her first humor column at age thirteen in the school newspaper; by high school she was writing for the *Dayton Herald*. She studied English at the University of Dayton, where she met her future husband Bill Bombeck. In 1949 she graduated from college, married Bill, and went to work as a reporter at the *Herald*. She quit in 1953 when she and Bill adopted a child, and became a full-time homemaker. Five years later she'd borne two babies, and was living the white picket fence dream—three kids, and a house in the suburbs.

She began writing about the daily reality of that dream—warts and all—when her youngest started school. Erma's modest, honest humor resonated with her audience—and by the next year her column was in syndication, and she was well on her way to becoming the nation's most popular humorist, writing two columns a week for more than seven hundred papers.

Erma was diagnosed with breast cancer in 1992. Her kidneys failed after her mastectomy surgery; in typical fashion she would not trade on her fame for a transplant. For four years she suffered through daily dialysis until receiving a kidney transplant. She died of complications after the surgery. She was sixty-nine.

bon mots

Erna Bombeck

" *I don't know why no one ever thought to paste a label on the toilet-tissue spindle giving 1-2-3 directions for replacing the tissue on it. Then everyone in the house would know what Mama knows.*

Giving birth is little more than a set of muscular contractions granting passage of a child. Then the mother is born.

Housework is a treadmill from futility to oblivion with stop-offs at tedium and counterproductivity.

How come anything you buy will go on sale next week?

*Marriage has no guarantees.
If that's what you're looking for, go live with a car battery.*

There is nothing more miserable in the world than to arrive in paradise and look like your passport photo.

*Mother's words of wisdom: 'Answer me!
Don't talk with food in your mouth!'*

God created man, but I could do better.

All of us have moments in our lives that test our courage.
Taking children into a house with white carpet is one of them.

Youngsters of the age of two and three are endowed with
extraordinary strength. They can lift a dog twice their own
weight and dump him into the bathtub.

Who, in their infinite wisdom, decreed that Little League
uniforms be white? Certainly not a mother.

People shop for a bathing suit with more care than they do
a husband or wife. The rules are the same. Look for something
you'll feel comfortable wearing. Allow for room to grow.

No self-respecting mother would run out of
intimidations on the eve of a major holiday.

On vacations: We hit the sunny beaches where we occupy
ourselves keeping the sun off our skin, the saltwater off our bodies,
and the sand out of our belongings.

Most children's first words are 'Mama' or 'Daddy.'
Mine were, 'Do I have to use my own money?'

Sometimes I can't figure designers out.
It's as if they flunked human anatomy.

*My theory on housework is, if the item doesn't multiply,
smell, catch on fire or block the refrigerator door, let it be.
No one cares. Why should you?*

*Before you try to keep up with the Joneses,
be sure they're not trying to keep up with you.*

*Have you any idea how many children it takes to turn
off one light in the kitchen? Three. It takes one to say,
'What light?' and two more to say, 'I didn't turn it on.'*

I never leaf through a copy of National Geographic
*without realizing how lucky we are to live in a society
where it is traditional to wear clothes.*

*When your mother asks, 'Do you want a piece of advice?'
it's a mere formality. It doesn't matter if you answer yes or no.
You're going to get it anyway.*

*A friend never defends a husband who gets his wife
an electric skillet for her birthday.*

A friend will tell you she saw your old boyfriend—and he's a priest.

*Anybody who watches three games of football in
a row should be declared brain dead.*

Being a child at home alone in the summer is a high-risk occupation. If you call your mother at work thirteen times an hour, she can hurt you.

Did you ever notice that the first piece of luggage on the carousel never belongs to anyone?

Don't confuse fame with success. Madonna is one; Helen Keller is the other.

Dreams have only one owner at a time. That's why dreamers are lonely.

For some of us, watching a miniseries that lasts longer than most marriages is not easy.

Great dreams never even get out of the box. It takes an uncommon amount of guts to put your dreams on the line, to hold them up and say, 'How good or how bad am I?' That's where courage comes in.

Guilt: the gift that keeps on giving.

Houseguests should be regarded as perishables: Leave them out too long and they go bad.

Housework, if you do it right, will kill you.

I come from a family where gravy is considered a beverage.

Humor is a spontaneous, wonderful bit of an outburst that just comes. It's unbridled, it's unplanned, it's full of surprises.

I have a hat. It is graceful and feminine and gives me a certain dignity, as if I were attending a state funeral or something. Someday I may get up enough courage to wear it, instead of carrying it.

I have a theory about the human mind. A brain is a lot like a computer. It will only take so many facts, and then it will go on overload and blow up.

I haven't trusted polls since I read that 62 percent of women had affairs during their lunch hour. I've never met a woman in my life who would give up lunch for sex.

I will buy any creme, cosmetic, or elixir from a woman with a European accent.

I'm going to stop punishing my children by saying, 'Never mind! I'll do it myself.'

I'm trying very hard to understand this generation. They have adjusted the timetable for childbearing so that menopause and teaching a sixteen-year-old how to drive a car will occur in the same week.

If you can't make it better, you can laugh at it.

I've exercised with women so thin that buzzards
followed them to their cars.

In two decades I've lost a total of 789 pounds.
I should be hanging from a charm bracelet.

It goes without saying that you should never have
more children than you have car windows.

Just think of all those women on the Titanic who said,
'No, thank you,' to dessert that night. And for what!

My second favorite household chore is ironing. My first being
hitting my head on the top bunk bed until I faint.

Myths that need clarification: 'Everyone in California lives on a white,
sandy beach.' False. The only people who live on California beaches are
vacationers from Arizona, Utah, and Nevada who own condos.

Never go to your high school reunion pregnant or they will think that is
all you have done since you graduated.

One thing they never tell you about child raising is that for
the rest of your life, at the drop of a hat, you are expected to
know your child's name and how old he or she is.

Never lend your car to anyone to whom you have given birth.

When humor goes, there goes civilization.

Thanksgiving dinners take eighteen hours to prepare.
They are consumed in twelve minutes.
Half-times take twelve minutes. This is not coincidence.

The only reason I would take up jogging is so that
I could hear heavy breathing again.

There is a thin line that separates laughter and pain,
comedy and tragedy, humor and hurt.

There is one thing I have never taught my body how to do and that
is to figure out at 6 A.M. what it wants to eat at 6 P.M.

There's nothing sadder in this world than to awake
Christmas morning and not be a child.

When a child is locked in the bathroom with water running and
he says he's doing nothing but the dog is barking, call 911.

When I stand before God at the end of my life,
I would hope that I would not have a single bit of
talent left and could say, 'I used everything you gave me.
"

THE PSYCHOLOGICAL BLONDE

Dr. Joyce Brothers

*Psychologist, Author,
TV/radio personality*
1928–

PLACE OF BIRTH:
New York City

GIVEN NAME:
Joyce Diane Bauer

BIRTHDAY:
September 20

SIGN:
Virgo

BLONDE MOMENT:
winning *The $64,000 Question*

CROWNING ACHIEVEMENT:
named one of the ten most
influential American women

BLONDO-BIOGRAPHY:
author of several books, including
Widowed and *What Every Woman
Needs to Know about Love and
Marriage*

Dr. Joyce Brothers is one of the most accomplished women of her generation—and one of the first to learn to play the media game. A New York City girl, she received her Ph.D. at Columbia University after graduating from Cornell.

Young and in need of money, she decided to win some on a game show. At the time the most popular show—and the one with the biggest purse—was *The $64,000 Question*. She chose the category of boxing, because she figured that the public would be intrigued by a feminine little blonde who knew everything there was to know about such a violent man's sport. She was right. After studiously tackling and memorizing all the trivia about the sport, she won a place on the show—and then took home the top prize of $64,000.

Her boxing acumen and media-genic personality led to a gig co-hosting NBC's *Sports Showcase*. This in turn led to her appearance on a number of television shows. Soon Joyce was America's psychologist—writing a daily syndicated newspaper column for more than 350 newspapers, doing radio five days a week for NBC, guest starring on TV shows of all stripes—from *Hollywood Squares* to *Late Night with Conan O'Brien*.

Through it all, she's remained a blonde. According to Dr. Joyce, we're conditioned to prefer the fair-haired at an early age. When drawing female stick figures, eighty percent of kindergartners color their hair blonde.

bon mots

“ *A strong, positive self-image is the best
possible preparation for success.*

*Accept that all of us can be hurt, that all of us can and surely
will at times fail. Other vulnerabilities, like being embarrassed
or risking love, can be terrifying, too. I think we should follow a
simple rule: If we can take the worst, take the risk.*

*Being taken for granted can be a compliment. It means that you've
become a comfortable, trusted element in another person's life.*

*Credit buying is much like being drunk. The buzz happens immediately
and gives you a lift. The hangover comes the day after.*

*I don't give advice. I can't tell anybody what to do.
Instead I say this is what we know about this problem at this time.
And here are the consequences of these actions.*

*Marriage is not just spiritual communion;
it is also remembering to take out the trash.*

Listening, not imitation, may be the sincerest form of flattery.

Trust your hunches. They're usually based on facts
filed away just below the conscious level.

The person interested in success has to learn to view failure as a healthy,
inevitable part of the process of getting to the top.

If Shakespeare had to go on an author tour to promote
Romeo and Juliet, *he never would have written* Macbeth.

Love comes when manipulation stops; when you think more
about the other person than about his or her reactions to you.
When you dare to reveal yourself fully. When you dare to be vulnerable.

No matter how lovesick a woman is,
she shouldn't take the first pill that comes along.

The best proof of love is trust.

The world at large does not judge us by who we
are and what we know; it judges us by what we have.

No matter how much pressure you feel at work,
if you could find ways to relax for at least
five minutes every hour, you'd be more productive. **99**

THE HITCHCOCK BLONDE

Grace Kelly

Actress and Princess of Monaco
1929–1982

PLACE OF BIRTH:
Philadelphia

BIRTH NAME:
Grace Patricia Kelly

NICKNAME:
Her Serene Highness

BIRTHDAY:
November 12

SIGN:
Scorpio

BLONDE MOMENT:
her 1956 "Wedding of the Century"
to Prince Rainier III of Monaco

CROWNING ACHIEVEMENT:
the crown of Monaco

BLONDO-BIOGRAPHY:
Grace, by official biographer
Robert Lacey

race Patricia Kelly may be the most well-named blonde of all time. The epitome of grace and beauty, the patrician Philadelphian was born into a rich and influential family. Despite their objections, the lovely debutante conquered New York and Hollywood first as a model, and then as an Academy Award-winning actress.

In her private life, however, the cool Grace was hot, hot, hot. It was during the Cannes Film Festival that Grace met the real-life prince who was to change her entire life. Prince Rainier of Monaco was the head of the House of Grimaldi, which had ruled the tiny principality since 1297. He needed a suitable Catholic wife, one who was as fertile as she was beautiful—for should he die without an heir Monaco would revert to France.

Who better than the Irish-American, good Catholic girl, Grace Kelly? Rainier loved her for her beauty and her celebrity; she loved him for his legendary charm and princely kingdom. Nine months and five days after their wedding, Princess Grace gave birth to her first child, Caroline. Forced to give up acting by her husband, Princess Grace devoted herself to her family and her adopted country. She had two more children, Albert and Stephanie, and worked tirelessly for charitable organizations, as well as the arts.

In a bizarre coincidence worthy of a Hitchcock film, Grace died on the same stretch of highway immortalized in *To Catch a Thief*, after suffering a stroke at the wheel. She was fifty-two.

BLONDE
bon mots

66 *The freedom of the press works in such a way that there is not much freedom from it.*

As an unmarried woman, I was thought to be a danger. Other women looked on me as a rival. And it pained me a great deal.

I don't want to dress up a picture with just my face. If anybody starts using me as scenery, I'll return to New York.

Women's natural role is to be a pillar of the family.

Emancipation of women has made them lose their mystery.

I don't want to be married to someone who feels inferior to my success or because I make more money than he does.

I don't like yelling and fighting, and I can't quarrel. Getting angry doesn't solve anything.

For a woman, forty is torture, the end.

I'll be goddamned if I'm going to stay in a business where I have to get up earlier and earlier and it takes longer and longer for me to get in front of a camera.

Hollywood amuses me. Holier-than-thou for the public and unholier-than-the-devil in reality.

I don't want to be married to someone who feels belittled by my success. I couldn't bear walking into a restaurant and hearing the maître d' refer to my husband as Mr. Kelly.

I hate to drive a car. I am not a good driver. **99**

THE STARLET BLONDE

Jayne Mansfield

Actress, Model, Beauty Queen
1933–1967

PLACE OF BIRTH:
Bryn Mawr, Pennsylvania

GIVEN NAME:
Vera Jayne Palmer

BIRTHDAY:
April 19

SIGN:
Aries

BLONDE MOMENT:
getting arrested for indecent
exposure in Vermont during
her nightclub act

CROWNING ACHIEVEMENT:
known as the poor man's
Marilyn Monroe

WEB SITE:
www.jaynemansfield.com

Vera was the pampered only child of a successful lawyer and his wife. When she was seventeen, she got pregnant and married Paul Mansfield—but that didn't stop her from pursuing her dream of stardom. She started taking acting courses, and eventually talked her husband into packing up baby Jayne Marie and moving to Hollywood.

Once there, her PR agent convinced Vera Jane to change her name to Jayne and dye her hair platinum blonde. With her forty-plus inch bust and her burning ambition, Jayne was quick to take advantage of every opportunity to promote herself—from "accidentally" losing her bikini top in the pool in front of lots of photographers to dying her poodles to match her outfits to tooling around town in her pink Jaguar. She never met a title she didn't like—Miss Negligee, Miss Nylon Sweater, Miss Freeway, Miss Geiger Counter, Miss Fourth of July, Miss Fire Prevention, Miss Tomato—until Miss Roquefort Cheese, which she declined.

Jayne never could escape the stereotypical dumb blonde image she had worked so hard to perfect. Since her death, she has become a cult figure of sorts, thanks to the larger-than-life persona she deliberately and carefully created to enhance her God-given pulchritude.

BLONDE
bon mots

❝ *I like nice things, but I've never accepted anything that I haven't earned.*

If I didn't have a large breast measurement, I'm sure people would talk about my small one. So what's the difference? I'm glad I have a large one. I don't mind at all when people stare at me. In fact, I love it. There isn't much point in trying to be glamorous if nobody will appreciate it.

The first step was to get all the men all stirred up. That's about completed. The next step is to get all the women stirred up. After that, I'll take a crack at the intellectuals.

I think being into yourself is wonderful, because then you can give so much of yourself to other people. One of my goals is to someday have my own billboard. People would see it and be a little happier.

Men are those creatures with two legs and eight hands.

Ever since I was a little girl, I was convinced I would be a star. I haven't got there yet, but I will. It's 80 percent determination and 20 percent talent.

I'm capable of creating true art through my talent and natural artistry. But Hollywood only wants me to show off my bust.

I think reviews are terribly, terribly unfair, and I can explain that. Reviews are terrible because they hurt actors, and reviews are also terrible because trees have to die to make that paper. You see?

Publicity can be terrible. But only if you don't have any.

The longer I'm around a man, the more likely he is to try something funny. Like they always say, familiarity breeds attempt.

My job is to appeal to everybody. Men look for sex appeal, women for identification, and children for a fairy story figure. I hope to get across all three.

Nothing risqué, nothing gained!

Stars were made to suffer, and I am a star.

We eat a lot of lean meat and fresh vegetables. You are what you eat, you know. When I'm 100 I'll still be doing pin-ups.

I like being a pin-up girl. There's nothing wrong with it.

A woman should be pink and cuddly for a man.

A forty-one inch bust and a lot of perseverance will get you more than a cup of coffee—a lot more. But most girls don't know what to do with what they've got.

It is the most wonderful feeling in the world, you know, knowing you are loved and wanted.

If you're going to do something wrong, do it big, because the punishment is the same either way.

Carrying a baby is the most rewarding experience a woman can enjoy.

I will never be satisfied. Life is one constant search for betterment for me. **99**

"Jayne Mansfield is making a career of being a girl."
— Walter Winchell

THE BIG-MOUTH BLONDE

Joan Rivers

Comedienne, Writer, Actress, Talk Show Host
1933–

PLACE OF BIRTH:

Brooklyn

GIVEN NAME:

Joan Alexandra Molinsky

NICKNAME:

Queen of the Barbed One-Liners

BIRTHDAY:

June 8

SIGN:

Gemini

BLONDE MOMENT:

her appearance as "Pepper January, Comedy with Spice" in a strip joint

CROWNING ACHIEVEMENT:

becoming Johnny Carson's permanent guest host

BLONDO-BIOGRAPHY

Author of the books, *Enter Talking, Bouncing Back, From Mother to Daughter*

WEB SITE:

www.joanrivers.com

Little Joan Molinsky was a natural blonde who wanted to be a movie star when she grew up. She realized that she could make people laugh, and from then on, her dream was to do just that. At Barnard she majored in English and anthropology—but her heart was on stage, where she performed in nearly all of the college productions.

Joan made the usual rounds of auditions in New York City, where she won roles in off-Broadway productions. Lenny Bruce encouraged her to do her own brand of brash comedy, and in 1965, after seven years of struggle, she finally got her big chance—an appearance on Johnny Carson's *Tonight Show.* Her career took off, and so did her love life. She met and married producer Edgar Rosenberg; in 1968 she gave birth to daughter Melissa.

In 1972 Joan moved her family to Los Angeles. There she wrote TV movies and feature films and became Johnny Carson's permanent guest host. She was comedy's golden girl—and then it all came crashing down around her. She alienated her mentor Carson when she signed on to do *The Late Show Starring Joan Rivers* on Fox TV without talking to him about it first; her husband had a heart attack; and the show was cancelled. As if that weren't enough, in 1987 her husband committed suicide.

The brash blonde from Brooklyn moved home. She got a new syndicated talk show—and won an Emmy, designed a line of jewelry, and was nominated for a Tony award. She's as brash as ever—and the public loves it.

BLONDE
bon mots

> *A man can sleep around, no questions asked, but if a woman makes nineteen or twenty mistakes she's a tramp.*

A woman went to a plastic surgeon and asked him to make her like Bo Derek. He gave her a lobotomy.

Before we make love my husband takes a pain killer.

Boy George is all England needs—another queen who can't dress.

Don't follow any advice, no matter how good, until you feel as deeply in your spirit as you think in your mind that the counsel is wise.

Don't tell your kids you had an easy birth or they won't respect you. For years I used to wake up my daughter and say, 'Melissa, you ripped me to shreds. Now go back to sleep.'

Forty for you, sixty for me. And equal partners we will be.

I blame my mother for my poor sex life. All she told me was 'the man goes on top and the woman underneath.' For three years my husband and I slept in bunk beds.

He who limps is still walking.

*I hate housework. You make the beds, you wash the dishes,
and six months later you have to start all over again.*

I have flabby thighs, but fortunately my stomach covers them.

*I knew I was an unwanted baby when I saw that my
bath toys were a toaster and a radio.*

*I told my mother-in-law that my house was her house, and she said,
'Get the hell off my property.'*

*I wish I had a twin, so I could know what
I'd look like without plastic surgery.*

If God wanted us to bend over he'd put diamonds on the floor.

*If we study the lives of great men and women carefully and
unemotionally we find that, invariably, greatness was developed,
tested, and revealed through the darker periods of their lives.*

Is Elizabeth Taylor fat? Her favorite food is seconds.

It's been so long since I've had sex I've forgotten who ties up whom.

My best birth control now is just to leave the lights on.

My mother could make anybody feel guilty—she used to get letters of apology from people she didn't even know.

My obstetrician was so dumb that when I gave birth he forgot to cut the cord. For a year that kid followed me everywhere. It was like having a dog on a leash.

My routines come out of total unhappiness. My audiences are my group therapy.

Never floss with a stranger.

Once you begin to believe there is help 'out there,' you will know it to be true.

Thank God we're living in a country where the sky's the limit, the stores are open late, and you can shop in bed thanks to television.

The first time I see a jogger smiling, I'll consider it.

There is not one female comic who was beautiful as a little girl.

I succeeded by saying what everyone else is thinking.

Can we talk? **99**

THE FEMINIST BLONDE
Gloria Steinem

Writer, Activist, Feminist
1934–

PLACE OF BIRTH:
Toledo, Ohio

GIVEN NAME:
Gloria Marie Steinem

BIRTHDAY:
March 25

SIGN:
Aries

BLONDE MOMENT:
her undercover stint as a *Playboy* bunny

CROWNING ACHIEVEMENT:
founder of the Ms. Foundation

BLONDO-BIOGRAPHY:
Author of the book *Revolution from Within*

WEB SITE:
www.msmagazine.com

Gloria started taking on challenges early in life. Her parents split up when she was only ten years old; with her father gone and her older sister off to college, little Gloria was left to care for her emotionally disturbed mother all by herself.

In Gloria's senior year of high school, her father agreed to take care of her mother for a year so Gloria could move in with her sister in Washington D.C. She went from there to her sister's alma mater Smith College, where Gloria found the supportive, nurturing environment she'd never had as a child. Here at this women's college she also discovered her love for politics and journalism.

Fueled by the realizations that her mother's unhappiness stemmed from her thwarted career ambitions and that her subsequent depression was trivialized because she was a woman, Gloria became an advocate for women's rights. She also began her career as a writer in the then all-male bastion of serious journalism (one *Life* magazine editor told her: "We don't want a pretty girl, we want a writer"). Her campaigning for women's rights led to her friendship with African-American activist Dorothy Pittman Hughes; with Hughes, she cofounded *Ms.* Magazine in 1972.

Since that time, Gloria has fought unceasingly for women's rights and has written several best-selling books—including the fascinating feminist look at another blonde, Marilyn Monroe, in *Marilyn: Norma Jean*.

bon mots

" *The first problem for all of us, men and women, is not to learn,
but to unlearn … as for logic, it's in the eye of the logician.*

If the shoe doesn't fit, must we change the foot?

*Writing is the only thing that, when I do it,
I don't feel I should be doing something else.*

*Power can be taken, but not given.
The process of the taking is empowerment in itself.*

*I have yet to hear a man ask for advice on
how to combine marriage and a career.*

The truth will set you free. But first, it will piss you off.

The authority of any governing institution must stop at its citizen's skin.

A pedestal is as much a prison as any small, confined space.

*Without leaps of imagination, or dreaming, we lose the excitement of
possibilities. Dreaming, after all, is a form of planning.*

*If women are supposed to be less rational and more emotional at
the beginning of our menstrual cycle when the female hormone is at
its lowest level, then why isn't it logical to say that, in those few days,
women behave the most like the way men behave all month long?*

*Law and justice are not always the same. When they aren't,
destroying the law may be the first step toward changing it.*

*Most women's magazines simply try to mold
women into bigger and better consumers.*

*We've begun to raise daughters more like sons...but few have
the courage to raise our sons more like our daughters.*

We can tell our values by looking at our checkbook stubs.

Most American children suffer too much mother and too little father.

I don't breed well in captivity.

*Childbirth is more admirable than conquest, more amazing
than self-defense, and as courageous as either one.*

Some of us are becoming the men we wanted to marry.

Most women are one man away from welfare.

A liberated woman is one who has sex before marriage and a job after.

Women may be the one group that grows more radical with age.

Someone asked me why women don't gamble as much as men do, and I gave the commonsensical reply that we don't have as much money. That was a true and incomplete answer. In fact, women's total instinct for gambling is satisfied by marriage.

A woman reading Playboy *feels a little like a Jew reading a Nazi manual.*

Planning ahead is a measure of class.
The rich and even the middle class plan for future generations, but the poor can plan ahead only a few weeks or days.

From pacifist to terrorist, each person condemns violence—and then adds one cherished case in which it may be justified.

No man can call himself liberal, or radical, or even a conservative advocate of fair play, if his work depends in any way on the unpaid or underpaid labor of women at home, or in the office.

The only thing I can't stand is discomfort.

Evil is obvious only in retrospect. 99

THE CONSERVATIONIST BLONDE

Jane Goodall

Scientist, Conservationist, Author
1934–

PLACE OF BIRTH:
London, England

GIVEN NAME:
Jane Goodall

BIRTHDAY:
April 3

SIGN:
Aries

BLONDE MOMENT:
invited the scorn of her peers when she named her chimps—instead of using numbers

CROWNING ACHIEVEMENT:
one of the world's leading conservationists

BLONDO-BIOGRAPHY:
Author of the books, *My Life with the Chimpanzees, In the Shadow of Man*

WEB SITE:
www.janegoodall.org

From the time she was a little girl, Jane was in love with nature. Entranced by everything African—from Tarzan to *The Jungle Book*—she knew from age eleven that she wanted to live in Africa when she grew up.

By the time she was in her early twenties, she made it to Africa. Bored with her secretarial job in Nairobi, she traveled to Zaire to meet famed anthropologists Louis and Mary Leakey. She signed on as their secretary, and was soon asked to take on chimpanzee research for a couple of years in Gombe, Tanzania.

So momentous was her work that Louis Leakey insisted that Jane get her Ph.D., so that her discoveries would be accepted within the academic and scientific communities. She was one of a handful of people without a college degree to receive a doctorate from Cambridge.

More than forty years later, Jane is still hard at work. The Director of Research at Gombe since 1967, Jane also works on behalf of her Jane Goodall Foundation, the Chimpanzee Guardian Project, and Roots & Shoots, which teaches kids about the environment. She's been honored in more ways than you can count—including the Albert Schweitzer Award, the Kyoto Prize for Science, and the Encyclopedia Britannica Award—but her greatest love remains her chimps.

bon mots

❝ *Only if we understand can we care. Only if we care
will we help. Only if we help shall all be saved.*

....

*It can seem as you look out that it's just chaos and that we
behave in terrible ways and we never really seem to get better.
But we have to remember that compassion and love and altruism
are equally deeply rooted in our primate heritage. We can push and
push and push towards love and compassion. That is where
I believe human destiny ultimately is taking us.*

....

*If you really want something, and really work hard, and take advantage
of opportunities, and never give up, you will find a way.*

....

*If you look through all the different cultures. Right from the
earliest, earliest days with the animistic religions, we have sought
to have some kind of explanation for our life, for our being, that is
outside of our humanity.*

....

*You cannot get through a single day without having an impact on the
world around you. What you do makes a difference, and you have to
decide what kind of difference you want to make.*

Chimpanzees have given me so much. The long hours spent with them in the forest have enriched my life beyond measure. What I have learned from them has shaped my understanding of human behavior, of our place in nature.

The least I can do is speak out for those who cannot speak for themselves.

When I left home and faced the realities of the world, I put my thoughts of God in cold storage for awhile, because I couldn't reconcile what I believed, deep inside, with what was going on around me. But that early period, when God was as real as the wind that blew from the sea through the pine trees in the garden; left me with inner peace, which, as I grew older, swelled— until, perforce, I had to open my mind to God again.

How would I have turned out, I sometimes wonder, had I grown up in a house that stifled enterprise by imposing harsh and senseless discipline? Or in an atmosphere of overindulgence, in a household where there were no rules, no boundaries drawn? My mother certainly understood the importance of discipline, but she always explained why some things were not allowed. Above all, she tried to be fair and to be consistent.

I wanted to talk to the animals like Dr. Doolittle.

It's easy to become hopeless. So people must have hope: the human brain, the resilience of nature, the energy of young people, and the sort of inspiration that you see from so many hundreds of people who tackle tasks that are impossible and never give up and succeed.

How we humans came to be the way we are is far less important than how we should act now to get out of the mess we have made for ourselves.

Our children are brutalized and insensitized if they are made to pull the spinal cord from a living frog : It will be that much easier, subsequently, to harm a dog, a chimpanzee—a human. Thus a more humane ethic—a respect for all living things—is desirable not only for the well-being of non-human animals, but for our own spiritual development as well.

Researchers find it very necessary to keep blinkers on...within the lab communities there is a very strong resistance among the researchers to admitting that animals have minds, personalities, and feelings.

I have a growing conviction that many animal data are not only obtained unethically, at huge cost in animal suffering, but are also unscientific, misleading, wasteful (in terms of dollars and effort) and may be actually harmful to humans.

That I did not fail was due in part to patience.

People say to me so often, 'Jane, how can you be so peaceful when everywhere around you people want books signed, people are asking these questions, and yet you seem peaceful,' and I always answer that it is the peace of the forest that I carry inside.

Especially now when views are becoming more polarized, we must work to understand each other across political, religious, and national boundaries.

We can't leave people in abject poverty, so we need to raise the standard of living for 80 percent of the world's people, while bringing it down considerably for the 20 percent who are destroying our natural resources.

Lasting change is a series of compromises. And compromise is all right, as long as your values don't change.

Thinking back over my life, it seems to me that there are different ways of looking out and trying to understand the world around us. There's a very clear scientific window. And it does enable us to understand an awful lot about what's out there. There's another window; it's the window through which the wise men, the holy men, the masters of the different and great religions look as they try to understand the meaning in **99** *the world. My own preference is the window of the mystic.*

THE FRENCH BLONDE

Brigitte Bardot

Actress, Animal Rights Activist, and Conservationist
1934–

PLACE OF BIRTH:
Paris

GIVEN NAME:
Camille Bardot

NICKNAME:
B.B.

BIRTHDAY:
September 28

SIGN:
Libra

BLONDE MOMENT:
the 1963 Cannes Film Festival, where the nubile new movie star caused an international sensation

CROWNING ACHIEVEMENT:
when the "phenomenon of nature" quit show business to found and run the Brigitte Bardot Foundation, an organization dedicated to protecting the rights of animals

BLONDO-BIOGRAPHY:
Her book, *Initiales B.B.*

WEB SITE:
www.foundationbrigittebardot.fr/uk

As any Frenchman would be happy to tell you, Brigitte Bardot is no ordinary blonde. In a country where blondes have long been celebrated, Brigitte is the raison d'etre of blondes. The child of an engineer and an ambitious housewife, Brigitte grew up in Paris. Her mother encouraged her youthful passion for singing and dancing. By fourteen, she was enrolled in the Conservatoire Nationale de Danse. A year later she graced the cover of *Elle* magazine, and a star was born. Famed French filmmaker Roger Vadim took one look and was hooked—the two became a couple, despite the fact that he was many years her senior.

Two years later she made her film debut in *Le Trou Normand* and married Vadim. Under the Svengali-like influence of Vadim, more movies followed—and in 1956, the twenty-four year old golden girl became an international sex symbol overnight with the film *And God Created Woman.*

Brigitte left Vadim not long afterwards, and a few years later married Jacques Charrier, with whom she had her only child, son Nicholas-Jacques in 1960. Her happiness was short lived, however. In 1962 she ended her marriage to Charrier. Ultimately, show business did not suit the sensitive, generous Brigitte. In 1973, at the age of thirty-nine, Brigitte quit making movies and devoted herself to crusading on behalf of animals and the environment.

When Brigitte makes headlines now, it is usually in reference to her activism—rather than her fabled sex appeal.

BLONDE
bon mots

" *I am the most important sex symbol of all time.*

(On first seeing Botticelli's *Birth of Venus*)
Was it me that Botticelli had in mind?

There is a French proverb: To live happy, live hidden.
Where can Brigitte Bardot hide?

I leave before being left. I decide.

I gave my beauty and my youth to men.
I am going to give my wisdom and experience to animals.

A photograph can be an instant of life captured for eternity that will
never cease looking back at you.

Every age can be enchanting, provided you live within it.

I don't think when I make love.

I have been very happy, very rich, very beautiful,
much adulated, very famous and very unhappy.

Women get more unhappy the more they try to liberate themselves.

I am leaving the town to the invaders: increasingly numerous, mediocre, dirty, badly behaved, shameless tourists.

I started out as a lousy actress and have remained one.

It is better to be unfaithful than to be faithful without wanting to be.

It is sad to grow old but nice to ripen.

Men are beasts and even beasts don't behave as they do.

I really wanted to die at certain periods in my life. Death was like love, a romantic escape. I took pills because I didn't want to throw myself off my balcony and know people would photograph me lying dead below.

I will never grow old until I stop growing up.

I really am a cat transformed into a woman. I purr. I scratch. And sometimes I bite. **"**

THE RADICAL BLONDE

Jane Fonda

Actress, Activist, Producer, Exercise Maven
1937–

PLACE OF BIRTH:
New York City

BIRTH NAME:
Jane Seymour Fonda

NICKNAME:
Hanoi Jane, Lady Jane

BIRTHDAY:
December 21

SIGN:
Sagittarius

BLONDE MOMENT:
appearing as the space-age blonde bimbo in *Barbarella*

CROWNING ACHIEVEMENT:
two Academy Awards, six Golden Globes, one Emmy, and five additional Oscar nominations

BLONDO-BIOGRAPHY:
Her autobiography, *My Life So Far*

WEB SITE:
www.jane-fonda.net

One of the most controversial blondes alive, Jane Fonda has played as many roles in life as she has in the movies. Born into Hollywood royalty, Jane is the daughter of film great Henry Fonda and socialite Frances Seymour Brokaw. Her privileged childhood was marked by her mother's death when Jane was twelve years old; she learned the true cause of her mother's death—suicide—when reading a magazine article.

The influence of the men in Jane's life has been profound. With first husband Roger Vadim she milked her blonde babeness—and promptly abandoned this role of playful vamp when she met second husband Tom Hayden. Hayden was an anti-war activist of the most serious kind, and with him at her side Jane took on more serious roles on and off-screen.

Even as she was lauded for her performances, she was vilified for her anti-war activities; considered a traitor by many Americans, she earned the pejorative nickname Hanoi Jane. But by the 1980s the Vietnam War was fading in people's memories, and Jane reinvented herself once again, cashing in on the aerobics craze with her best-selling series of exercise videos. Her marriage to Tom Hayden ended in 1990; in 1991 she married media tycoon Ted Turner and retired from acting.

They divorced after ten years. Jane has since written her memoirs and returned to acting.

BLONDE
bon mots

" *Working in Hollywood does give one a certain expertise in the field of prostitution.*

I was terrified when I turned thirty. I was pregnant and had the mumps and Faye Dunaway was just coming out in Bonnie and Clyde *(1967). I thought, 'Oh my God, I'll never work again. I'm old!'*

(Talking about her 1962 film *Walk on the Wild Side*)
Acting with [Laurence] Harvey is like acting by yourself—only worse.

(Expressing regret at her support for the Viet Cong)
It hurt so many soldiers. It galvanized such hostility. It was the most horrible thing I could possibly have done. It was just thoughtless.

I, a socialist, think we should strive toward a socialist society, all the way to communism.

(Speaking to students at the University of Michigan in 1970)
If you understood what communism was, you would hope, you would pray on your knees that one day we would become communist.

It's never too late—never too late to start over, never too late to be happy.

I thank God and I thank Ted Turner (her estranged husband)
everyday that I don't have to make movies.

I'm perfect. The areas that I need help on are not negotiable.
They have to do with gravity.

You can do one of two things; just shut up, which is something I don't
find easy, or learn an awful lot very fast, which is what I tried to do.

When you can't remember why you're hurt, that's when you're healed.

(On America, 2003)
I don't know if a country where the people are so ignorant of
reality and of history, if you can call that a free world.

I'm really appalled by plastic surgery in this country.
We've got to make friends with those sags and wrinkles,
as they represent our lifetime experience.

You spend all your life trying to do something
they put people in asylums for.

A good many dramatic situations begin with screaming.

If the career you have chosen has some unexpected inconvenience,
console yourself by reflecting that no career is without them.

A man has every season while a woman only has the right to spring.

(On being an actor)
I'm an assistant storyteller. It's like being a waiter or a gas-station attendant, but I'm waiting on six million people a week, if I'm lucky.

Ted needs someone to be there 100 percent of the time. He thinks that's love. It's not love—it's babysitting.

Telling lies and showing off to get attention are mistakes I made that I don't want my kids to make.

To be a revolutionary you have to be a human being. You have to care about people who have no power.

To the man who only has a hammer, everything he encounters begins to look like a nail.

We cannot always control our thoughts, but we can control our words, and repetition impresses the subconscious, and we are then master of the situation.

Women are not forgiven for aging. Robert Redford's lines of distinction are my old-age wrinkles.

"

THE LIVING BLONDE
Martha Stewart

Stockbroker, Caterer, Writer,
TV Personality, Entrepreneur
1941–

PLACE OF BIRTH:
Nutley, New Jersey

BIRTH NAME:
Martha Helen Kostyra

BIRTHDAY:
August 3

SIGN:
Leo

BLONDE MOMENT:
selling that ImClone stock

CROWNING ACHIEVEMENT:
founder of Martha Stewart Living
Omnimedia

BLONDO-BIOGRAPHY:
The blonde behind *Martha Stewart
Living* and a series of books

WEB SITE:
www.marthastewart.com

The story of little Martha Kostyra from Nutley, New Jersey is a cautionary tale for blondes everywhere. One of six children raised by working-class Polish immigrants, Martha was well-schooled in the domestic arts as a child. A good student, Martha won a partial scholarship to prestigious Barnard College upon her graduation from Nutley High School—and never looked back.

An attractive blonde, Martha worked as a model. She married law student Andrew Stewart in 1961, and in 1965 gave birth to her only child Alexis. Martha gave up modeling, and became one of the country's first female stockbrokers in 1968. She and her husband bought and restored a nineteenth century farmhouse in Connecticut—and she found her calling. Martha started a catering business and began writing articles on cooking, gardening, and decorating. She divorced her husband in 1990, and celebrated with the debut of her magazine *Martha Stewart Living* that same year; a wildly successful syndicated TV show of the same name followed in 1993. Martha branched out into home products, more television, and the Internet.

Now one of the wealthiest self-made women in America, Martha ran a billion-dollar company and hobnobbed with the rich and famous. But after a controversial trial, in which Martha did not take the stand in her own defense, she was convicted of four felony charges: conspiracy to obstruct justice, make false statements, and commit perjury; two counts of false statements; and obstruction of justice.

❝ *You know, in China they say, 'The thinner the chopsticks, the higher the social status.' Of course, I got the thinnest I could find...that's why people hate me.*

The most loved of all pies in America is the old-fashioned apple pie.

It's a good thing.

I catnap now and then, but I think while I nap, so it's not a waste of time.

I was married for thirty years. Isn't that enough? I've had my share of dirty underwear on the floor.

I have a lot of energy.

My tastes may have gotten a little better, or a little bit more educated. But still, I always get up and clean out the kitty litter.

Americans look at you very differently, respect you greatly more when you write a book.

My dream was to be an eclectic knowledge-gathering person.

*We're not so free that we don't have to listen to rules,
and laws, and regulations.*

(When asked about the ImClone scandal
on national television, while she was slicing vegetables)
I'm going to concentrate on my salad.

*I want you to know that I am innocent—and
that I will fight to clear my name.*

*I love this company, its people, and everything it stands for, and I am
stepping aside as Chairman and CEO because it is the right thing to do.*

*I am obviously distressed by the jury's verdict, but I continue to take
comfort in knowing that I have done nothing wrong and that I have the
enduring support of my family and friends. I will appeal the verdict
and continue to fight to clear my name. I believe in the fairness of the
judicial system and remain confident that I will ultimately prevail.*

I'm very sad. **99**

THE CHANEL BLONDE
Catherine Deneuve

Actress, Singer
1943–

PLACE OF BIRTH:
Paris

GIVEN NAME
Catherine Dorleac

BIRTHDAY:
October 22

SIGN:
Libra

BLONDE MOMENT:
she was the model for Marianne, the symbol of France who appears on French coins and stamps

CROWNING ACHIEVEMENT:
she's a grande dame of French film

WEB SITE:
www.cdeneuve.com

atherine Dorleac was born into a family of actors and didn't waste any time getting into the business. The third of four daughters, she made her film debut at thirteen in *The Twilight Girls* in 1956, taking her mother's maiden name Deneuve. Over the next few years, Catherine would expand her range, perfecting her "ice maiden" image.

As elegant in real life as she is in reel life, Catherine has long been an icon of Gallic style. She was Yves Saint-Laurent's muse—and still wears his clothes today. As the face of Chanel, she graced billboards and magazines and commercials for many years—and as a result became as well-known in America as she was in her native country. The perfume *Deneuve* is named in her honor.

As a woman of a "certain age," as the French say, Catherine is as beautiful and sexy as ever—and still in demand as an actress. She returned to musicals in *8 Femmes* and *Dancer in the Dark*; in addition to her film work, she also appears in TV movies and mini-series. Although Catherine has always preferred to work close to home, she is nonetheless an international star.

BLONDE
bon mots

Sexuality is such a part of life,
but sexuality in movies—I have a hard time finding it.

People who know me know I'm strong, but I'm vulnerable.

I'm lucky. I'm getting older with some directors who are getting older.

I don't see any reason for marriage when there is divorce.

To work is a noble art.

A star remains pinned on a wall in the public imagination.

From the start, marriage was instituted for contemptible,
practical reasons—an idea of men.

I have always been sensitive to the kindness
of people in general, and men in particular.

I have never borne a grudge against any man whom I've loved.
All the men I've had in my life are unique and irreplaceable.

If I'm working, I prefer persuasion. In love, I prefer charm.

*A woman's life is a little like a mountain—with two slopes.
As soon as you've reached the top of one side,
you have to go back down the other.*

*I am not a saint, I suffer just like the rest of the world.
You never know where passion is going to take you.*

I do not consider myself beautiful. Pretty, maybe, but not beautiful.

*At forty-five you are not beautiful in the same way
that you were at twenty-five. You need to find the
character, the personality—that allows others to*
"
regard you well. That's tougher if you were beautiful.

MOTHER & DAUGHTER BLONDES

Goldie Hawn

Dancer, Actress, Producer
1945–

PLACE OF BIRTH:
Washington. D.C.

GIVEN NAME:
Goldie Jean Studlendegehawn

BIRTHDAY:
November 21

SIGN:
Scorpio

BLONDE MOMENT:
worked as a can-can girl at the 1965 World's Fair

CROWNING ACHIEVEMENT:
one Best Supporting Actress Oscar and one Best Actress Oscar nomination

Kate Hudson

Actress
1980–

PLACE OF BIRTH:
Los Angeles

GIVEN NAME:
Kate Garry Hudson

BIRTHDAY:
April 19

SIGN:
Aries

BLONDE MOMENT:
ditched college to go straight into acting

CROWNING ACHIEVEMENT:
her break-out role as rock groupie Penny Lane in *Almost Famous*

Goldie Hawn and Kate Hudson are without a doubt the cutest and most talented blonde mother and daughter in Hollywood. Goldie became America's sweetheart in the 1960s. She oozed bubble-headed charm. After appearing as a dancer in Disney's *The One and Only, Genuine, Original, Family Band* (where she first met longtime companion Kurt Russell), she stole the show right out from under legends Walter Matthau and Ingrid Bergman in 1969's *Cactus Flower*. She's tackled a variety of roles since—from the serious to the campy to the sublime.

Married three times, Goldie is the mother of three—Oliver and Kate Hudson (fathered by former husband Bill Hudson), and Wyatt Russell (fathered by longtime live-in love Kurt Russell).

Daughter Kate is by all accounts as adorable as her mother—and as talented. Kate caught the acting bug early; after several small roles in indie films, she talked writer/director Cameron Crowe into casting her in his rock-and-roll homage *Almost Famous.* Kate won a Golden Globe and an Oscar nomination for Best Supporting Actress for her winsome performance.

Kate married former Black Crowes singer Chris Robinson in 2000; on January 7, 2004, Kate made Goldie a grandmother when she gave birth to son Ryder Russell Robinson. The mother/daughter team also plans to make movies together.

GOLDIE

(In 1977)

66 *Monogamy is impossible these days for both sexes.*
I don't know anyone who's faithful or wants to be.

Men are much simpler mechanisms than women. Nothing changes them...even when they have a midlife crisis, they do it in a mindless way. That's why I think we should let men go off and have affairs and drive fast cars and dream of being virile—and we should run the world.

I must say that the biggest lesson you can learn in life, or teach your children, is that life is not castles in the skies, happily ever after. The biggest lesson we have to give our children is truth. We're all built with illusions. And they break.

I have witnessed the softening of the hardest of hearts by a simple smile.

How long can you be cute?

There are only three ages for women in Hollywood—Babe, District Attorney, and Driving Miss Daisy.

Once you can laugh at your own weaknesses, you can move forward. Comedy breaks down walls. It opens up people. If you're good, you can fill up those openings with something positive. Maybe you can combat some of the ugliness in the world.

I've finally stopped running away from myself. Who else is there better to be?

KATE

I'm superstitious…but not like wear-the-same-underwear-for-two-weeks superstitious.

I have a big, flamboyant, open personality, which I think is why people may be saying these nice things about me.

Sometimes I'll be walking down the street [in Paris] and I'll hear some American and I'll just go, 'Of course they hate us, of course they can't stand us. We're the most annoying, boisterous creatures in the world.' I mean we come in and we eat mounds of food, and we're like, 'Where's the ketchup for our French fries.' I'm like, 'Shut up.'

I have zero problems when people say, 'God, you look like your mother.' I go, 'Well, great! Thanks!' **"**

THE COUNTRY BLONDE
Dolly Parton

Singer, Songwriter, Actress
1946–

PLACE OF BIRTH:
Sevier County, Tennessee

GIVEN NAME:
Dolly Rebecca Parton

BIRTHDAY:
January 19

SIGN:
Capricorn

BLONDE MOMENT:
getting the implants that made her country's bustiest star

CROWNING ACHIEVEMENT:
the most famous female country singer of all time

BLONDO-BIOGRAPHY:
Her books, *Dolly: My Life and Other Unfinished Business*, *Coat of Many Colors*

WEB SITE:
www.dollywood.com

Dolly Parton grew up on a tobacco farm in the Smoky Mountains, one of twelve children in a one-room cabin with no electricity or indoor plumbing. But there was plenty of music—Dolly was making up songs before she could read or write. By age eleven, she was singing at a Knoxville radio station, and made her first recording for the small label Gold Band Records. By 1967 she had her first hit single—"Dumb Blonde"—and a spot on Porter Wagoner's popular TV show.

Together over the next seven years, Dolly and Porter recorded fourteen top ten hits—including "The Last Thing on My Mind" and "Please Don't Stop Loving Me." But Dolly was an independent young woman and eventually struck out on her own. By 1976 she had her own show, *Dolly*, and numerous Country Music Association awards. The very next year she added a Grammy for Best Female Country performance for "Here You Come Again." Her screen debut in *Nine to Five* won her an Oscar nomination for the title song of the same name, which she wrote and performed.

A savvy businesswoman, Dolly has parlayed her larger-than-life persona and talent into a $100 million media empire, Dolly Parton Enterprises. Her amusement parks, Dollywood and Dollywood's Splash Country, draw millions of visitors each year to Pigeon Forge, Tennessee. Dolly continues to write and record songs, to act, and to tour. Smart, lively, and irrepressible, Dolly is the modern Mae West, country-style.

66 *I hated school. Even to this day, when I see a school bus it's just depressing to me. The poor little kids.*

I'm not offended by dumb blonde jokes because I know that I'm not dumb. I also know I'm not blonde.

*I look just like the girls next door...
if you happen to live next door to an amusement park.*

I modeled my looks on the town tramp.

I was the first woman to burn my bra—it took the fire department four days to put it out.

I'm not going to limit myself just because people won't accept the fact that I can do something else.

If you talk bad about country music, it's like saying bad things about my momma. Them's fightin' words.

My aunt in Knoxville would bring newspapers up, which we used for toilet paper. Before we used it, we'd look at the pictures.

My husband said 'show me your boobs' and I had to pull up my skirt...so it was time to get them done!

My weaknesses have always been food and men—in that order.

People make jokes about my bosoms; why don't they look underneath the breasts at the heart? It's obvious I've got big ones, and if people want to assume they're not mine, then let them.

Plastic surgeons are always making mountains out of molehills.

Storms make trees take deeper roots.

Yeah I flirt, I'm not blind, and I'm not dead!

You'd be surprised how much it costs to look this cheap!

You'll never do a whole lot unless you're brave enough to try.

The way I see it, if you want the rainbow, you gotta put up with the rain.

Find out who you are and do it on purpose.

I describe my look as a blend of Mother Goose, Cinderella, and the local hooker!

I like to buy clothes that are two sizes too small
and then take them in a little.

I have little feet because nothing grows in the shade.

If you don't like the road you're walking, start paving another one.

I had to get rich so I could afford to sing like I was poor again.

There are plenty of charities for the homeless.
Isn't it time somebody helped the homely?

I don't know if I'm supporting them, or they're supporting me.

People always ask me if they're mine.
Yes, they are...all bought and paid for.

If I build another park, it will probably be in Silicon Valley.

99

Hillary Rodham Clinton

Lawyer, Author, First Lady, Senator

1947–

PLACE OF BIRTH:

Chicago

GIVEN NAME:

Hillary Diane Rodham

BIRTHDAY:

October 26

SIGN:

Scorpio

BLONDE MOMENT:

marrying the law student from Arkansas

CROWNING ACHIEVEMENT:

first sitting First Lady to win an elected office

BLONDO-BIOGRAPHY:

Her book, *Living History*

WEB SITE:

http://clinton.senate.gov/

Little Hillary Rodham was a smart, bespectacled girl who was recognized early on as one of the best and the brightest of a newly liberated generation of feminist women. Generally acknowledged as the kind of woman who could become the first female president, she mortified friends and mentors alike in 1975 when she put her own ambitions on the back burner, married fellow law student Bill Clinton, and moved to his home state of Arkansas. She did not take his name.

Hillary gave birth to their only child, Chelsea, in 1980. Husband Bill had political ambitions; he followed up a stint as Attorney General with his run for Governor. Under public pressure, she took Clinton's name, lost weight, switched from glasses to contact lenses, and started wearing more fashionable, feminine clothes. And she went blonde.

The farther up the political ladder Bill climbed, the blonder Hillary got. With his election to the presidency, she became one of the most powerful First Ladies in history. Her worst time in the White house came with the Monica Lewinsky scandal and its aftermath. Hillary stood fast as the power wife whose sleek, controlled blondness contrasted with her rival's dark, youthful sexuality.

The blonde won. Long after Monica Lewinsky has been forgotten, the reign of Hillary Rodham Clinton continues. Coming full circle, Senator Hillary Rodham Clinton is now the first name mentioned when the possibility of the first female president is raised.

BLONDE
bon mots

" *I'm not some little woman, 'standing by my man,'*
like Tammy Wynette.

There really is a vast right-wing conspiracy—my only regret was in using the word 'conspiracy'—there's definitely nothing secret about it.

If I want to knock a story off the front page, I just change my hairstyle.

I have said that I'm not running and I'm having a great time pre—being a first-term senator.

I consider myself a New Democrat. I am very proud of the political identity developed by Democrats during the Clinton administration.

I have to confess that it's crossed my mind that you could not be a Republican and a Christian.

We are the president.

The challenge now is to practice politics as the art of making what appears to be impossible, possible.

There cannot be true democracy unless women's voices are heard.
There cannot be true democracy unless women are given
the opportunity to take responsibility for their own lives.
There cannot be true democracy unless all citizens are
able to participate fully in the lives of their country.

The challenges of change are always hard. It is important
that we begin to unpack those challenges that confront this nation
and realize that we each have a role that requires us to change and
become more responsible for shaping our own future.

In the Bible it says they asked Jesus how many times
you should forgive, and he said seventy times seven.
Well, I want you all to know that I'm keeping a chart.

I have gone from a Barry Goldwater Republican to a New Democrat,
but I think my underlying values have remained pretty
constant; individual responsibility and community.
I do not see those as being mutually inconsistent.

I have met thousands and thousands of pro-choice men and women.
I have never met anyone who is pro-abortion. Being pro-choice is not
being pro-abortion. Being pro-choice is trusting the individual to make
the right decision for herself and her family, and not entrusting that
decision to anyone wearing the authority of government in any regard.

Eleanor Roosevelt understood that every one of us every day has choices to make about the kind of person we are and what we wish to become. You can decide to be someone who brings people together, or you can fall prey to those who wish to divide us. You can be someone who educates yourself, or you can believe that being negative is clever and being cynical is fashionable. You have a choice.

When I am talking about 'It Takes a Village,' I'm obviously not talking just about or even primarily about geographical villages any longer, but about the network of relationships and values that do connect us and bind us together.

No government can love a child, and no policy can substitute for a family's care. But at the same time, government can either support or undermine families as they cope with moral, social, and economic stresses of caring for children.

I'm sick and tired of people who say that if you debate and disagree with this administration, somehow you're not patriotic. We need to stand up and say we're Americans, and we have the right to debate and disagree with any administration.

Our lives are a mixture of different roles. Most of us are doing the best we can to find whatever the right balance is....For me, that balance is family, work, and service.

I wasn't born a first lady or a senator. I wasn't born a Democrat. I wasn't born a lawyer or an advocate for women's rights and human rights. I wasn't born a wife or a mother.

God bless the America we are trying to create. **99**

THE ACTRESS BLONDE
Meryl Streep

Actress
1949–

PLACE OF BIRTH:
Summit, New Jersey

BIRTH NAME:
Mary Louise Streep

NICKNAME:
Meryl Sheep (on *Sesame Street*)

BIRTHDAY:
June 22

SIGN:
Cancer

BLONDE MOMENT
in high school, the awkward teen
got contact lenses and dyed her hair
blonde and became a cheerleader
and homecoming queen

CROWNING ACHIEVEMENT
nominated for the Academy Award
a record-breaking thirteen times,
and won it twice—so far

WEB SITE:
www.merylstreeponline.net,
www.meryl-streep.de/meryl/

For every joke about dumb blondes, for every wisecrack about ditzy blonde actresses, for every snide remark about dyed blonde sirens, there is one supreme retort: Meryl Streep. As brilliant as she is beautiful, as balanced as she is blonde, Meryl Streep is arguably our greatest living film actress. But more than that, she is a mother and wife and an artist, who brings an integrity to everything she does. This integrity informs and illuminates her work as it does her life.

Since her first Oscar win in 1979 for *Kramer vs. Kramer*, Meryl has gone on to build one of the most successful careers in Hollywood, winning our admiration and respect in wildly divergent performances—from the suicidal concentration camp survivor in *Sophie's Choice* (for which she won a second Academy Award, this one for Best Actress in a Lead Role) to her multi-role tour de force in HBO's *Angels in America*. Just as important, she has built a happy personal life as well, as wife and mother of four. Blondes don't come any smarter—or classier—than Meryl Streep.

BLONDE
bon mots

66 *Motherhood has a very humanizing effect.*
Everything gets reduced to essentials.

Instant gratification is not soon enough.

You can't get spoiled if you do your own ironing.

I have always regarded myself as the pillar of my life.

It's bizarre that the produce manager is more
important to my children's health than the pediatrician.

Integrate what you believe in every single area of your life. Take your
heart to work and ask the most and best of everybody else, too.

I would like to spank director Spike Jonze.

Expensive clothes are a waste of money.

Every single decision I make about what material I do,
what I'm putting out in the world, is because of my children.

I was never the kind of person who said, 'I'm going to be an actress. And if I meet somebody and have a family, great.' I always, always, since I was a little girl, wanted to have kids and a family. I just had to wait thirty years to find somebody I liked enough.

Listening is everything. And I mean that in terms of before you work, after you work, in between work, with your children, with your husband, with your friends, with your mother, with your father. It's everything. And it's where you learn everything.

If I had any advice for young actors or actresses—especially actresses, because men have a lot more freedom in this area—it's to establish early on that you're going to send vanity away. Send it packing.

I've always felt older. I've always felt about forty [and] I did have this moment when I turned forty that I felt like my clothes finally fit. And I didn't have to be anything other than myself.

I've never wanted to fit myself into that sort of iconography of 'movie star' or something. I've never wanted to be any bigger than I am as a human being.

Acting is a clearing away of everything except what you want and need—and it's wonderful in that way—and when it's right, you're lost in the moment. **"**

THE BRASH BLONDE
Cybill Shepherd

Model, Actress, Singer
1950–

PLACE OF BIRTH:
Memphis, Tennessee

GIVEN NAME:
Cybill Lynne Shepherd

BIRTHDAY:
February 18

SIGN:
Pisces

BLONDE MOMENT
voted Miss Congeniality at the
Miss Teenage America pageant

CROWNING ACHIEVEMENT:
her campy turn as Martha Stewart
in the TV movie *Martha, Inc.*

BLONDO-BIOGRAPHY:
Her book, *Cybill Disobedience*

WEB SITE:
www.cybill.com

The beautiful blonde tomboy from Memphis was breaking hearts and winning beauty contests right out of puberty. At sixteen, Cybill took home a year's supply of Dr. Pepper and a brand-new wardrobe from Sears when she was crowned Miss Teenage Memphis. Her modeling career took off—and soon her face was gracing the covers of high-fashion magazines everywhere. Famed director Peter Bogdanovich saw that face on the cover of *Glamour* and fell in love. He cast her as the small-town seductress in *The Last Picture Show*. Her affair with Bogdanovich earned her the ire of Hollywood and her next several movies were flops.

Cybill went home to Memphis, married local boy David Ford, and had a baby, daughter Clementine in 1980. Three years later, she starred in the short-lived TV series *The Yellow Rose*, which led to the plum role of Maddy Hayes in the hit series *Moonlighting*. Cybill married again, this time to Bruce Oppenheim, with whom she had twins Ariel and Zachariah, and then starred in her own sitcom *Cybil*. As the spokesperson for L'Oreal Preference she spoke for all blondes when she tossed her trademark locks and told America, "Because I'm worth it."

❝ *I think the measure of your success to a certain extent will
be the amount of things written about you that aren't true.*

(On *The Last Picture Show*)
*When a film wraps, the actors often like to keep some of their
props or wardrobe as mementos. I wanted the heart-shaped locket and
brown and white saddle shoes that Jacy wore, but (Bogdanovich's wife)
Polly was in charge of costumes and wouldn't give them to me. I guess
she figured I had enough of a souvenir: her husband.*

*I had the serendipity of modeling during a temporary interlude
between Twiggy and Kate Moss, when it was actually okay for
women to look as if we ate and enjoyed life.*

*We have to keep trying things we're not sure we can pull off.
If we just do the things we know we can do…you don't grow as much.
You gotta take those chances on making those big mistakes.*

Living together is so much sexier than being married.

Therapy helps you. I went through the baggage.

(On motherhood)
I got baby fever at twenty-eight.

I'm not blonde to be more fun; I'm blonde because it looks better.

I took what I wanted.

(On sex)
I was completely unprepared for the pleasure I would experience.

I was definitely a tomboy.
I wanted to wear overalls for the rest of my life.

There's been so much press [saying] that I'm a monster. I'm not. **99**

THE LUSTY BLONDE

Kim Cattrall

Actress, Author
1956–

PLACE OF BIRTH:
Liverpool, England

GIVEN NAME:
Clare Woodgate

BIRTHDAY:
August 21

SIGN:
Leo

BLONDE MOMENT:
her turn as the sex-crazed gym teacher in *Porky's*

CROWNING ACHIEVEMENT:
boosting the sex appeal of older women everywhere

BLONDO-BIOGRAPHY:
Her book, *Satisfaction: The Art of the Female Orgasm*

L ittle Clare Woodgate was born in England. Raised in Canada, at eleven the precocious performer was off to the homeland to study at the London Academy of Music and Dramatic Art. After renaming herself Kim Cattrall, she made a number of films, but her first taste of fame came with a series of sexy roles in sophomoric, but successful comedies, namely *Porky's*, *Police Academy*, and *Mannequin*.

Along the way, the attractive brunette dated high-profile men and married three times. But her greatest success came as a blonde, in the wildly popular HBO TV series, *Sex and the City*. As the unapologetically rapacious Samantha Jones, Kim showed the world that women over forty were the sexiest, most self-assured women around.

Ironically, Samantha's sexual expertise was not borne of Kim's own experience. Admitting that she'd long suffered an inability to experience orgasm, she and third husband Mark Levinson wrote a book designed to help other women experience sexual pleasure. Not surprisingly, *Satisfaction: The Art of the Female Orgasm* has been a best-seller.

Whatever Kim Cattrall does next, she'll be an inspiration to women of all ages to be their sexy, most adventurous selves.

bon mots

> *People assume that for me to play a sexually open character like Samantha, I must have had fabulous sex for most of my life.*

I've been playing sexually aware women most of my life. At this point I expected to be playing moms and wives. It's exciting to play a femme fatale.

There are so many avenues of performing. I'm not interested in the form of musical theater unless it's something like Rocky Horror Picture Show, *which is a blast.*

I don't know many women who can relate to Sharon Stone and the kind of movies she does. I don't know a lot of guys who can relate to Tom Cruise's movies because they're on a kind of fantastic level. I like movies I can relate to.

The show [Sex and the City] *is celebrating what it's like to be a woman. We do things people think about but don't vocalize. It gives men and women permission to talk in a way that is healthy.*

I'm making choices that I think fit me better than a sort of pie-in-the-sky plan that I thought I should follow. I feel good about that.

It [Crossroads] was one of the hardest jobs in my life. I had to be mean to Britney Spears. She is such a little Southern sweetie who is only twenty. She was so nervous and so well-prepared, and I had to reject her on-screen because I'm her horrible mother who has left her.

Sure she [Samantha] wants great sex. But what she really wants is to be held in the morning. I think that's what makes her character empathetic. She has a really big heart, and she wants to be loved.

I think that forty looks different than it did when my mother was forty. I eat well, I exercise, and I'm much more conscious of what's going on in my life.

It's no real mystery that women of a certain age tend not to exist in Hollywood. Before this show [Sex and the City], I was dealing with that. There were no roles for forty year olds, and if there was, it went to Michelle Pfeiffer. I love Michelle, but what about the rest of us?

It [imagination] helps me to become part of that journey that I'm going through in front of the camera, or in front of an audience. I used to think you had to disappear within a character, but I find that puts a mask on what I do.

I think the wonderful thing about doing theater is that it's more of an actor's medium. I think that film is more of a director's medium. You can't edit something out on stage. It's there. ,,

THE FUNNY BLONDE
Ellen DeGeneres

Comedienne, Actress, Activist, Talk Show Host
1958–

PLACE OF BIRTH:
Metairie, Louisiana

GIVEN NAME:
Ellen Lee DeGeneres

BIRTHDAY:
January 26

SIGN:
Aquarius

BLONDE MOMENT:
wearing the promise ring her boyfriend gave her in high school

CROWNING ACHIEVEMENT:
coming out on national television

BLONDO-BIOGRAPHY:
Her books, *The Funny Thing Is,* and *My Point…and I Do Have One* and *Love, Ellen* (by Ellen's mother Betty DeGeneres)

WEB SITE:
www.ellen.warnerbros.com

Ellen spent her early life in the New Orleans area—and loved it. When her parents split up and she moved with her mom to small-town Atlanta, Texas, it was a whole new world for her. She graduated from high school in 1976 and wasted no time moving back to New Orleans. Her goal was to appear on Johnny Carson's *Tonight Show*.

She got her big break in 1982; after being named Louisiana's Funniest Person, she competed in the national competition, and won the title of Funniest Person in America. She then moved to San Francisco, and joined the comedy scene there. Here she caught the eye of Budd Friedman of L.A.'s famous Improv comedy club, who encouraged her to move south. After opening for Jay Leno at the Improv, Leno recommended her to Johnny Carson—and the moment in the spotlight that she'd dreamed about came true.

This led to work in TV, but it wasn't until 1994 that Ellen finally got her own show. Originally called *These Friends of Mine*, the show was re-titled *Ellen* for the second season. Popular with viewers from the start, the show made history in 1997 with *The Puppy Episode*, in which Ellen came out of the closet on national television. The fateful episode won critical raves and an Emmy for Ellen. By 2003 she was taking daytime television by storm with her new talk show, *The Ellen DeGeneres Show*, and in love with new squeeze Alexandra Hedison. Which just goes to prove that you can't keep a funny blonde down for long.

bon mots

Ellen DeGeneres

66 *I think they should have a Barbie with a buzz cut.*

I'm a godmother, that's a great thing to be, a godmother.
She calls me God for short, that's cute, I taught her that.

I was coming home from kindergarten—well, they told me it was
kindergarten. I found out later I had been working in a factory for ten
years. It's good for a kid to know how to make gloves.

In the beginning there was nothing. God said, 'Let there be light!'
And there was light. There was still nothing, but you could see it
a whole lot better.

Normal is getting dressed in clothes that you buy for work and
driving through traffic in a car that you are still paying for—in order to
get to the job you need to pay for the clothes and the car, and the house
you leave vacant all day so you can afford to live in it.

I'm a lesbian, an Aquarian, and a vegetarian.

People always ask me 'Were you funny as a child?'
Well, I was an accountant.

I was raised around heterosexuals, as all heterosexuals are.
That's where us gay people come from—you heterosexuals.

(On her love scene with Bill Pullman in *Mr. Wrong*)
It's a combination of Something Wild, After Hours,
and Mary Poppins*...if Mary Poppins were naked.*

The sixties were when hallucinogenic drugs were really, really big.
And I don't think it's a coincidence that we had the
type of shows we had then like The Flying Nun.

I ask people why they have deer heads on their walls.
They always say because it's such a beautiful animal. There you go.
I think my mother is attractive, but I have photographs of her.

My grandmother started walking five miles a day when she was sixty.
She's ninety-seven now, and we don't know where the hell she is.

You say you're sick and tired of hearing about me?
I've got news for you: I'm sick and tired of hearing about me.

(On hosting the Emmy's, November 4, 2001)
What would bug a guy from the Taliban more than seeing a gay
woman in a suit surrounded by Jews?

99

Giving birth is like taking your lower lip and forcing it over your head.

THE MATERIAL BLONDE
Madonna

Singer, Composer, Producer,
Actress, Author
1958–

PLACE OF BIRTH:

Bay City, Michigan

GIVEN NAME:

Madonna Louise Veronica
Ciccone

NICKNAME:

Nonnie

BIRTHDAY:

August 16

SIGN:

Leo

BLONDE MOMENT:

when she kissed sister blonde
Britney Spears

CROWNING ACHIEVEMENT:

she's one of the most successful pop
artists in history

BLONDO-BIOGRAPHY:

Her book, *Sex*

WEB SITE:

www.madonna.com

No natural brunette has capitalized more on her adopted blondness than Madonna. The queen of reinvention has used her hair color to define and redefine herself time and time again over the last twenty years.

She began as a dancer, moving to New York and studying with Alvin Ailey in the late 1970s. By the early 1980s, she was singing with a number of dance bands in the underground dance club scene. She scored her first hit with the dance club single "Everybody." From there it was one "Holiday" after another—and by the time her second LP brought "Like a Virgin" and "A Material Girl" to an eager public, Madonna was a household name.

Since that time, Madonna has sold some 200 million albums worldwide. The one thing they've had in common is novelty—Madonna changes personas the way other blondes change lipsticks. She's been every blonde there is: the Marilyn Monroe look-alike; the *Dick Tracy* femme fatale Breathless Mahoney; the *Blonde Ambition* pop mogul; the rags-to-riches Evita Peron, the *Truth or Dare* libertine; the *Ray of Light* spiritual seeker, the *Music* cowgirl, even the prim English storytelling "mum." Along the way she's given birth to two children, recorded more than twenty-five Top Ten singles, published the best-selling children's books *The English Roses* and *Mr. Peabody's Apples*, and collected three Grammy Awards, a Golden Globe award, countless lovers, two husbands, and some $650 million.

BLONDE
bon mots

" *I'm anal retentive. I'm a workaholic. I have insomnia. And I'm
a control freak. That's why I'm not married. Who could stand me?*

I always thought of losing my virginity as a career move.

*I wouldn't have turned out the way I was if I didn't have
all those old-fashioned values to rebel against.*

*I stand for freedom of expression, doing what you believe in,
and going after your dreams.*

I won't be happy till I'm as famous as God.

*Effeminate men intrigue me more than anything in the world.
I see them as my alter egos. I feel very drawn to them.
I think like a guy, but I'm feminine. So I relate to feminine men.*

*Everyone probably thinks that I'm a raving nymphomaniac, that I have
an insatiable sexual appetite, when the truth is I'd rather read a book.*

*Sometimes I look back at myself and remember things
I used to say, or my hairstyle, and I cringe.*

I always thought I should be treated like a star.

I suppose I sometimes used to act like I wasn't a human being... I'm not interested in being Wonder Woman in the delivery room.
Give me drugs.

I'm tough, I'm ambitious, and I know exactly what I want.
If that makes me a bitch, okay.

If I was a girl again, I would like to be like my fans,
I would like to be like Madonna.

My father was very strong. I don't agree with a lot of the ways he brought me up. I don't agree with a lot of his values, but he did have a lot of integrity, and if he told us not to do something, he didn't do it either.

Poor is the man whose pleasures depend on the permission of another.

There are moments when I can't believe I'm as old as I am.
But I feel better physically than I did ten years ago. I don't think,
Oh God, I'm missing something.

I became an overachiever to get approval from the world.

To me, the whole process of being a brushstroke in
someone else's painting is a little difficult.

Catholicism is not a soothing religion. It's a painful religion.
We're all gluttons for punishment.

I sometimes think I was born to live up to my name.
How could I be anything else but what I am having been named
Madonna? I would either have ended up a nun or this.

I don't think you can ever love enough.

Because I've taken my clothes off in public doesn't
mean that I've revealed every inch of my soul.

I wanted to do everything everybody told me I couldn't ever do.

It's a great feeling to be powerful. I've been striving for it all of my life.
I think that's just the quest of every human being. Power.

Someday I'm going to live out, in real life, my greatest sexual fantasy—
seducing a priest, on stage, live, in front of twenty-five thousand people.

Straight men need to be emasculated. I'm sorry. They all need to be
slapped around. Women have been kept down for too long. Every straight
guy should have a man's tongue in his mouth at least once.

Ever since my daughter was born, I feel the fleetingness of time.
And I don't want to waste it on getting the perfect lip color.

Madonna is my real name. It means a lot of things.
It means virgin, mother, mother of earth, someone who is
very pure and innocent but someone who's very strong.

Many people see Eva Peron as either a saint or the incarnation of Satan.
That means I definitely can identify with her.

I miss New York. I still love how people talk to you on the street—just
assault you and tell you what they think of your jacket.

I would like to see the Pope wearing my T-shirt.

I wanted to be a nun. I saw nuns as superstars.
When I was growing up, I went to a Catholic school, and the nuns,
to me, were these superhuman, beautiful, fantastic people.

If I weren't as talented as I am ambitious,
I would be a gross monstrosity.

Being loved keeps you young.

When I'm hungry, I eat. When I'm thirsty, I drink.
When I feel like saying something, I say it.

Children always understand. They have open minds.
They have built-in shit detectors.

I think that everyone should get married at least once,
so you can see what a silly, outdated institution it is.

I feel just as hungry today as I did the day I left home.

Better to live one year as a tiger, than a hundred as sheep.

I am my own experiment. I am my own work of art.

To be brave is to love someone unconditionally, without expecting
anything in return. To just give. That takes courage, because
we don't want to fall on our faces or leave ourselves open to hurt. **99**

THE PRINCESS BLONDE
Diana

Princess, Fashion Icon, Activist
1961–1997

PLACE OF BIRTH:
Park House, near Sandringham

BIRTH NAME
Diana Francis Spencer

NICKNAME:
Queen of Hearts

BIRTHDAY:
July 1

SIGN:
Cancer

BLONDE MOMENT:
her wedding to Charles,
Prince of Wales, making her
the first Englishwoman to
marry an heir to the throne in
more than three hundred years

CROWNING ACHIEVEMENT:
breathing life and humanity
into a stuffy, boring royal family

BLONDO-BIOGRAPHY:
Andrew Morton's *Diana*

WEB SITE:
www.althorp.com

Every little girl in the United Kingdom grows up dreaming of marrying a prince. For little Diana Francis Spencer, who grew up playing with the Prince of Wales' little brothers, that dream seemed more appropriate for her older sisters. But Charles, twelve years Diana's senior, was too busy playing the field to settle on any of the beautiful women who doted on him. By the time Diana was old enough to date, Charles was, as Jane Austen might say, "in need of a wife." Diana was deemed suitable, and the seduction began.

Lucky for Charles, Diana was quick to provide him with the obligatory "heir and a spare," giving birth to two sons in rapid succession, William Arthur Louis in 1982 and Henry Charles Albert David in 1984. Despite the appearance of a happy family, Diana and Charles were not the ideal couple the royal family pretended they were. In fact, Charles touched off the inevitable decline of their union by flaunting his love for former girldriend, Camilla Parker-Bowles. Devastated, Diana took solace in her sons, her charity work, and lovers of her own. Charles and Diana divorced in 1996.

In 1997 Diana fell in love with Dodi Fayed. Their affair attracted intense public attention, and the relentless following of the paparazzi. While trying to escape such attention, they were both killed in a car accident in Paris. The world mourned the loss of the "People's Princess," and still mourns today. Princess Diana redefined what it means to be a princess.

BLONDE
bon mots

" *Any sane person would have left long ago. But I cannot. I have my sons.*

Anywhere I see suffering, that is where I want to be, doing what I can.

Being a princess isn't all it's cracked up to be.

Call me Diana, not Princess Diana.

Carry out a random act of kindness, with no expectation of reward,
safe in the knowledge that one day someone might do the same for you.

Everyone needs to be valued.
Everyone has the potential to give something back.

Everyone of us needs to show how much we care for each
other and, in the process, care for ourselves.

Helping people in need is a good and essential part of my life,
a kind of destiny.

HIV does not make people dangerous to know, so you can shake their
hands and give them a hug : Heaven knows they need it.

Hugs can do great amounts of good—especially for children.

I am not a political figure, nor do I want to be one;
but I come with my heart.

I don't even know how to use a parking meter, let alone a phone box.

I don't go by the rule book—I lead from the heart, not the head.

I don't want expensive gifts; I don't want to be bought.
I have everything I want. I just want someone to be there for me,
to make me feel safe and secure.

I have a woman's instinct and it's always a good one.

I like to be a free spirit. Some don't like that, but that's the way I am.

I think the biggest disease the world suffers from in this day
and age is the disease of people feeling unloved. I know that
I can give love for a minute, for half an hour, for a day, for a month,
but I can give. I am very happy to do that, I want to do that.

I understand people's suffering, people's pain,
more than you will ever know yourself.

I'd like people to think of me as someone who cares about them.

I'd like to be a queen in people's hearts,
but I don't see myself being queen of this country.

I'm as thick as a plank.

If men had to have babies, they would only ever have one each.

People think that at the end of the day a man is the only answer.
Actually, a fulfilling job is better for me.

So many people supported me through my public life
and I will never forget them.

The greatest problem in the world today is intolerance.
Everyone is so intolerant of each other.

The kindness and affection from the public have carried
me through some of the most difficult periods,
and always your love and affection have eased the journey.

There were three of us in this marriage, so it was a bit crowded.

You can't comfort the afflicted without afflicting the comfortable.

It's vital the monarchy keeps in touch with the people.
It's what I try and do.

*I knew what my job was; it was to go out and
meet the people and love them.*

*I will fight for my children on any level so they can reach
their potential as human beings and in their public duties.*

*I think like any marriage, especially when you've had divorced parents
like myself, you'd want to try even harder to make it work.*

*At the age of nineteen, you always think you are
prepared for everything and you think you* **"**
have the knowledge of what's coming ahead.

THE "BAYWATCH" BLONDE
Pamela Anderson

Actress, Producer,
Animal Rights Activist
1967–

PLACE OF BIRTH:

Ladysmith, British Columbia,
Canada

BIRTH NAME:

Pamela Denise Anderson

NICKNAME:

Pammy

BIRTHDAY:

July 1

SIGN:

Cancer

BLONDE MOMENT:

marrying rocker Tommy Lee
ninety-six hours after meeting him

CROWNING ACHIEVEMENT:

receiving the Linda McCartney
Award for her animal rights activism

BLONDO-BIOGRAPHY:

The National Enquirer's *Pam*

WEB SITE:

www.pamelaanderson.com

Pamela Anderson has been a star since the day she was born—literally. As the first baby born in her native Canada on its centennial celebration, she was christened the "Centennial Baby" and became a household name. Her fame was secured some twenty years later, when she was caught on camera at a British Columbia Lions football game wearing a LaBatt's beer T-shirt, causing a sensation. Overnight she became the Blue Zone spokeswoman for LaBatt's beer, which led to more work in commercials as well as her first *Playboy* cover. She's since appeared on the cover of *Playboy* magazine more often than any other woman in history.

Pamela's blonde charm proved a double whammy with her twin TV debut roles—as Lisa the Tool Time Girl on Tim Allen's popular sitcom *Home Improvement* and as C.J. Parker in the international smash hit *Baywatch*. Working two jobs was too tough—and eventually Pamela left *Home Improvement* to focus on being the *Baywatch* blonde.

A long-time vegetarian, she's also a dedicated and energetic animal rights activist. In 1999, she received the Linda McCartney Award for her work on behalf of animals. She's also branching out professionally—appearing in such feature films as *Scary Movie*, inspiring the lead character in the animated series *Stripperella*, writing a column for *Jane* magazine, and launching her own line of clothing. Whatever she does, she brings her own brand of blondness to bear—and makes her mark.

BLONDE
bon mots

66 *I don't really think about anything too much.*
I live in the present. I move on. I don't think about what
happened yesterday. If I think too much, it kind of freaks me out.

Making love in the morning got me through morning sickness.
I found I could be happy and throw up at the same time.

What I know in life runs the gamut of the 'feminist experience.'
The true meaning of feminism is this: to use your strong womanly
image to gain strong results in society.

I have this phobia: I don't like mirrors. And I don't watch
myself on television. If anything comes on, I make them shut it off,
or I leave the room.

I'm a mother with two small children,
so I don't take as much crap as I used to.

My ideal relaxation is working on upholstery.
I spend hours in junk shops buying furniture. I do all the
upholstery work myself, and it's like therapy.

It's great to be a blonde.
With low expectations it's very easy to surprise people.

Tattoos are like stories—they're symbolic of the important
moments in your life. Sitting down, talking about where you
got each tattoo and what it symbolizes, is really beautiful.

There's never going to be a great misunderstanding of me.
I think I'm a little whacked.

There's no way I set out to be a certain kind of symbol—the way
I dress is the way I am, the way I live my life.

In junior high, a boy poured water down my shirt and yelled:
'Now maybe they'll grow.'

(On the lap dancer's pole in her bedroom)
My sons think it's a fireman's pole, but I forgot
to cut a hole through the ground into the kitchen. **99**

THE SMALL-TOWN BLONDE

Renee Zellweger

Actress
1969–

PLACE OF BIRTH:

Katy, Texas

GIVEN NAME:

Renee Kathleen Zellweiger

NICKNAME:

Zelly

BIRTHDAY:

April 25

SIGN:

Taurus

BLONDE MOMENT:

at the Golden Globe Awards, when they called out her name as Best Actress—and she was in the bathroom

CROWNING ACHIEVEMENT:

stealing the hearts of all those Brits who pooh-poohed her casting as Bridget Jones in *Bridget Jones's Diary*

Renee Zellweger is a small-town girl—and proud of it. Born and raised in Katy, a small town some thirty miles outside of Houston, Renee lived a conventionally rural life—complete with "pigs and horses and cows and chickens down the street." Yet the Texas native was not just like the other cheerleaders and drama clubbers and track athletes she grew up with. She went to the University of Texas in Austin to study English, determined to become a writer. But she caught the acting bug instead. The success of *Love and a .45*, in which she played a gun-toting trailer trash moll, finally led her to Los Angeles.

In 2001 she outraged the United Kingdom when she took on the beloved Bridget Jones character for the film version of the international best-seller *Bridget Jones's Diary*—but twenty pounds and a British accent later she'd won over all but her fiercest critics and picked up an Oscar nomination.

But it was her heartbreaking turn as the feisty Ruby Thewes in *Cold Mountain* that would win her the Academy Award for Best Actress in a Supporting Role.

Cold Mountain proved lucky for her in other ways as well. Jack White played Ruby's love interest—and that love has bloomed off-screen as well as on-screen. For this small-town blonde with big ambitions, dreams do still sometimes come true.

(On Los Angeles)

❝ *It opens your eyes in this town, it's amazing.*
It's taught me who I don't want to be.

(On the set of *Cold Mountain* in Romania)

I learned how little in the way of material goods we really need,
and how beautiful a simple life can be. In Romania, people
work with their hands every day, and you'll see an eighty-year-old
woman still chopping wood because she's been looking after herself
all her life, and she still has the strength to do it.

This [my backside] is still very, very big.

Being horrible in a big film is a quicker nosedive than
doing an obscure film and making no money.

(On playing Roxie Hart in *Chicago*)

She's so earnest in a way, and so desperate and tragic in another.
She's so desperate for fame because of what she thinks it will bring—
self-esteem, self-respect, self-worth, love. All the things she doesn't have
a lot of. She feels that if she is lionized by the masses like Velma, she'll
be more whole as a person. The sad reality is that it's a fallacy.

*I'm getting better at dealing with fame, I guess.
But I still feel stupid. I mean, if I were Stephen Hawking,
then you could come up to me and tell me I'm great.*

*I'm hugely embarrassed when it comes to scatological matters,
and I'm very shy about my sexuality.*

*I can't control what people think...it's [what's written about her]
going to be read by however many millions of people and I can't
meet all those people and explain the circumstances about my life.*

I'm sick of talking about myself. In fact, I'm tired of talking.

*I've always known who I am in terms of what brings me happiness,
and that's not negotiable.*

I don't want to be somebody else or do what somebody has already done.

*I'm a dork. That's the truth. I'm a dork and the idea that
I'm in a movie with Tom Cruise is hysterical. It really is.*

(On learning to dance for Chicago)
*Learning a whole new medium of expression yourself is so fulfilling in
ways that I never imagined. I feel more present than I have in my life
for so long as a result of this. To use your body in that way, to express
yourself in that way...I shouldn't even try to explain it, because I can't.*

*It diminishes your worth as a person and your character,
to some degree, if you're willing to share your greatest intimacies
with people you've never met.*

---

*When a woman stands naked in a room,
unless that particular moment is held up by the subject matter,
all you notice is that there's a naked girl.*

---

*I was happy to look down and see these big thighs and cellulite.
I loved it. It was truly liberating. There's so much room to think
about other things when you're not thinking about your body.*

---

*On a superficial level, I'm clumsy, self-deprecating,
uncertain at times, and I say stupid things.*

---

*I'm not that self-aware. I don't spend my day thinking,
'Hmm, how am I being perceived today?'
I don't have time for that. I have a lot of great friends to call instead.*

99

Renee Zellweger

THE COOL BLONDE
Gwyneth Paltrow

Actress
1972–

PLACE OF BIRTH:
Los Angeles

GIVEN NAME:
Gwyneth Kate Paltrow

NICKNAME:
Gwynnie

BIRTHDAY:
September 28

SIGN:
Libra

BLONDE MOMENT:
voted "Most Stuck Up" by Movieline

CROWNING ACHIEVEMENT:
winning the Oscar for playing a girl
pretending to be a boy pretending
to be a girl in *Shakespeare in Love*

BLONDO-BIOGRAPHY:
Daniel O'Brien's *Gwyneth Paltrow*

Gwyneth Paltrow was born into show business. The daughter of Tony-award-winning actress Blythe Danner and director/producer Bruce Paltrow, she spent much of her childhood in the Berkshires, hanging out with her parents while they did summer stock. She made her debut there in a production of *The Adventures of Huckleberry Finn*. In 1991, she won a small role in the film *Shout*, and followed that up with a number of small parts in movies that included *Flesh and Bone* and *Jefferson in Paris*.

Her roles as the title characters in *Emma* and Michael Douglas's better half in *The Perfect Murder* led to her Oscar-winning role as Violet in Tom Stoppard's *Shakespeare in Love*.

After a series of celebrated relationships with the likes of Brad Pitt and Ben Affleck, Gwyneth has now paired up with Chris Martin of the band Coldplay. They were married secretly in 2003. They had their first child, a baby girl named Apple Blythe Alison Martin, in May 2004. Although Gwyneth has been quoted as saying she's ready to concentrate on "partners and babies," we're betting that she'll return to the screen, balancing motherhood and career with the same aplomb her mother has done.

bon mots

" Beauty, to me, is about being comfortable in your own skin.
That, or a kick-ass red lipstick.

....

I don't really understand the concept of having a career,
or what agents mean when they say they're building one for you.
I just do things I think will be interesting and that have integrity.
I hate those tacky, pointless, big, fluffy, unimportant movies.

....

I try to remember, as I hear about friends getting engaged,
that it's not about the ring. It's a grave thing, getting married.

....

(On her 1997 break-up with Brad Pitt)
It really changed my life. When we split up, something changed,
permanently, in me. My heart sort of broke that day, and it
will never be the same.

....

(On her father's struggle with cancer)
It changed me more than anything else. You don't want to get
to that place where you're the adult and you're palpably in the
next generation. And, this shoved me into that.

People have become inappropriate. People have pushed too far. People have climbed one too many fences. I'm just tired of it.

I find Sex and the City *irreverent and shocking. It's one step beyond how girls really talk. I would do a cameo on that show in a flash.*

I'm glad that some day my children will be able to see my father and hear his voice, get a sense of who he was. One of the things that disturbs me the most about the fact that he's dead is that I feel like a statistic. I sort of feel like one of those people who was unfortunate and lost their father when they were thirty, and life goes on. But he was so unique and so incredible, I don't like to think about it in those terms.

I worked so much in my twenties, and I really burnt the candle at both ends. I wasn't too picky about what I did, and I was lucky that I did some really good films, but I also did some really rubbish films. I think part of the downside about being so successful and winning the Oscar at the age of twenty-six is that I sort of became insouciant about the things that I chose. I thought 'Oh, I'll just try this, it'll be fun, or I'll do that for the money…' Things like that now I would absolutely never do.

I don't want to be rich, and I don't want to be famous.

I used to be super-trusting. But in my position, that doesn't get you very far these days.

I realized life is so short and precious, you should do things that make you feel inspired, that push you and teach you something. I'd rather not have a big house, a huge closet of clothes, diamonds and a private plane, and instead a body of work that I'm proud of.

I just have no more bad habits to give up.

I love men, even though they're lying, cheating scumbags.

In Los Angeles everyone has perfect teeth. It's crocodile land. **99**

Gwyneth Paltrow

THE NO-HOLDS BARRED BLONDE

Drew Barrymore

Actress, Producer
1975–

PLACE OF BIRTH:

Culver City, California

GIVEN NAME:

Drew Blythe Barrymore

NICKNAME:

"D"

BIRTHDAY:

February 22

SIGN:

Pisces

BLONDE MOMENT:

when she posed as Marilyn Monroe
on the cover of JFK Jr.'s *George*
magazine in honor of Bill Clinton's
fiftieth birthday

CROWNING ACHIEVEMENT:

getting her own star on the
Hollywood Walk of Fame, along
with relatives Ethel, John, and
Lionel Barrymore

BLONDO-BIOGRAPHY:

Her autobiography, *Little Girl Lost*

If anyone was born to the Hollywood life, it's Drew Barrymore. By the age of eleven months, the granddaughter of noted thespian John Barrymore had joined the family business of acting with the debut of her first Puppy Chow commercial. By her adorable turn in *ET*, she was America's darling.

Within just a few years, however, it looked like Drew might suffer the same fate shared by many a child star. The product of a broken home, with two unconventional parents beset by their own problems, Drew fell into drinking and drugs. But then she went into rehab, pulled herself together, and revealed all in *Little Girl Lost*, a no-holds-barred autobiography detailing her substance abuse and recovery.

Reinventing herself as a sexpot, she shed her child star image for that of titillating vamp in such films as *Poison Ivy*, *The Amy Fisher Story*, and *Batman Forever*. Drew completed her treacherous transition from child star to Hollywood powerhouse with the *Charlie's Angels* movies—in which she served as producer as well as star. The films—which have made more than $500 million worldwide—have made Drew one of Tinseltown's most successful producers. Whatever happens, you know that this blonde Barrymore will not only survive, she'll flourish.

BLONDE
bon mots

❝ *There's something liberating about not pretending.*
Dare to embarrass yourself. Risk.

If I ever start talking to you about my 'craft,' my 'instrument,'
you have permission to shoot me.

I believe in fate. I believe that everything happens for a reason, but I
think it's important to seek out that reason—that's how you learn.

Every morning I stay in bed for ten minutes to ponder my place in the
universe; then I wash my face and check my karma.

God made a very obvious choice when he made me voluptuous;
why would I go against what he decided for me? My limbs work,
so I'm not going to complain about the way my body is shaped.

I am obsessed with ice cubes. Obsessed.

I don't want to be stinky poo poo girl, I want to be happy flower child.

I know certain actors are totally screwed up on drugs, yet it gets
covered up. Why wasn't I excused for 'exhaustion' or 'the flu'?

I get to be a kid now, because I wasn't a kid when I was supposed to be one. But in some ways, I'm like an old woman—lived it, seen it, done it, been there, have the T-shirt.

I learned early on that family, as far as my mother and father, were not an option.

My favorite book when I was eight was Everything You Always Wanted to Know About Sex—But Were Afraid to Ask. *I was not afraid to ask.*

I pray to be like the ocean, with soft currents, maybe waves at times. More and more, I want the consistency rather than the highs and the lows.

I used to look in the mirror and feel shame, I look in the mirror now and I absolutely love myself.

I want people to be blown away when I do what they don't expect.

I've always said that one night, I'm going to find myself in some field somewhere: I'm standing on grass, and it's raining, and I'm with the person I love, and I know I'm at the very point I've been dreaming of getting to.

I've been a vegetarian for years and years. I'm not judgmental about others who aren't, I just feel I cannot eat or wear living creatures.

If you're going to go through hell…
I suggest you come back learning something.

Kissing—and I mean like, yummy, smacking kissing—is the
most delicious, most beautiful and passionate thing that two
people can do, bar none. Better than sex, hands down.

Love is the hardest habit to break, and the most difficult to satisfy.

My whole life, I've wanted to feel comfortable in my skin.
It's the most liberating thing in the world.

Oh, I love hugging. I wish I was an octopus,
so I could hug ten people at a time!

Sometimes I bust out and do things so permanent.
Like tattoos and marriage.

When I lay my head on the pillow at night I can say
I was a decent person today. That's when I feel beautiful.

When you've been locked up in a mental
institution, people are going to ask questions. 99

THE SOUTHERN BLONDE
Reese Witherspoon

Actress
1976–

PLACE OF BIRTH:
Baton Rouge, Louisiana

GIVEN NAME:
Laura Jeanne Reese Witherspoon

BIRTHDAY:
March 22

SIGN:
Aries

BLONDE MOMENT:
the ad she did for Gap adorned
a six-story building on Sunset
Boulevard

CROWNING ACHIEVEMENT:
winning the National Society of Film
Critics award for Best Actress

BLONDO-BIOGRAPHY:
Ursula Rivera's *Reese Witherspoon*

WEB SITE:
www.rwitherspoon.com

For many girls, being a Southern blonde is a double whammy—if they thought you were a dumb blonde before, just wait till they hear that drawl. But Reese Witherspoon has turned that stereotype on its head, playing the not-as-dumb-as-I-look blonde to the hilt, and laughing all the way to the bank.

The daughter of a surgeon and pediatric nurse, Reese was educated at a private girls' school and at Stanford University. She started acting as a "hobby," but started taking her career more seriously in 1991 when cast in *The Man in the Moon*. She became America's newest blonde sweetheart in 2001 when she appeared as Elle Woods in *Legally Blonde*, the sorority girl from Beverly Hills who chases her man to the ends of the earth—Harvard—to try and win him back. Reese served as executive producer of the sequel, *Legally Blonde 2*, which has made nearly as much as the original.

Lest you think that Reese is blessed only in the career department, think again. She married heartthrob Ryan Phillippe in 1999; they have two children, daughter Ava and son Deacon. Reese brings an intelligent insouciance to all she does—proving that what they say about Southern charm is true, especially if you're blonde.

" (On having a baby)
*Obviously, this isn't the time in my life that
I would have chosen to do this, but I feel like life gives you
these challenges for a reason…I really feel blessed.*

*I'm lucky to find a person to share my life,
and the best friend I'll ever have.*

*The battles that we face in this business aren't financial,
but they are moral.*

*I just don't see myself as the girl that everybody likes.
I never have been and I don't know how to be that person.*

*Oh, I was kind of the slut of fifth grade when I was twelve. I kissed a boy
in a roller-rink and none of my girlfriends could believe I'd done it.*

*Don't even get me started about Hollywood actors or
actresses—they're so arrogant. Around here, talent gets you into
parties, it gets you great tables at restaurants, obviously it gets you
great dates. But it takes a long time to understand that ultimately,
it doesn't make you a good person.*

*I'm always shocked when I meet most movie stars and realize that they
are normal people who have normal houses and live normal lives.*

*Being a Southern person and a blonde, it's not a good
combination. Immediately when people meet you,
they think of you as not being smart.*

*Attending an all-girls school has its advantages,
there are no inhibitions. You can walk to school with your
zit cream on and your hair in rollers and nobody cares.*

*I like people laughing at me. I'd much rather hear someone say,
'Oh, you look kind of funny' than 'Oh, you're so pretty.'*

*(About being a young mother)
I knew there were going to be people who'd say,
'You have a career' or 'You're young.'
But nobody who knows me would ever say those things to me.*

*I see these young women who are so overtly sexual. The pictures
they pose for, and the outfits they wear, with their boobs pushed
up like earmuffs. And it's like, that's wonderful now, hon, when you
are twenty years old, but what will you do when you are thirty-five
and your boobs don't want to go that way anymore?*

If acting didn't work out for me, I could be a professional trampolinist.

*It isn't always easy seeing your boyfriend, like, you know,
in a bathtub with some girl or kissing some other girl.*

*Many people worry so much about managing their careers, but rarely
spend half that much energy managing their lives. I want to make my
life, not just my job, the best it can be. The rest will work itself out.*

You're always just one movie away from not being in Vogue anymore.

*I've argued with lots of directors, because they pay you to come in and
give your two cents about your character. It's going to be you up there on
the screen and you should know better than anybody what you're doing.*

*There was a girl in junior high. She was so perfect. She had
all the boyfriends and was the smartest girl in school. And she was
rude to me! This is my little revenge. I'm doing her in Election.*

*I have a weird process, but the main thing is like this:
I hear her [the character's] voice in my head. There are a
lot of wonderful scripts my agents can't believe I pass on,
but I do because I can't hear the voice. It doesn't appeal to me then.
I'm really careful. Unless I hear the voice, I can't do it.*

I grew up in Tennessee. We didn't know what Louis Vuitton was.
I had to order all my prom outfits out of catalogs.

It's nice to come home to what's real. **99**

THE BUBBLEGUM BLONDE
Britney Spears

Singer, Actress
1981–

PLACE OF BIRTH:
Kentwood, Louisiana

GIVEN NAME:
Britney Jean Spears

NICKNAME:
Brit, Pinkey

BIRTHDAY:
December 2

SIGN:
Sagittarius

BLONDE MOMENT:
voted a "Fun and Fearless female"
by *Cosmopolitan* magazine

CROWNING ACHIEVEMENT:
leading pop star of her generation

BLONDO-BIOGRAPHY:
Britney Spears, A Mother's Gift
(co-authored with her mother)

WEB SITE:
www.britneyspears.com

There are child stars, and there are child stars, and then there's Britney Spears. Her parents Lynne and Jamie indulged their little blonde daughter's love of the spotlight, sending her to dance lessons and gymnastics classes. But despite her success in these other arenas, what Britney really longed to do was sing. At eleven, she auditioned for the *New Mickey Mouse Club.* Landing this role, she took her place among a cast of Mouseketeers as talented and ambitious as she.

But Britney left her squeaky clean Disney image behind in the late 1990s when she signed as a Jive Recording Artist. Her album *Baby One More Time* debuted in 1999—and Britney became an overnight sensation worldwide. The new pop star played the role of diva to the hilt—appearing in her underwear on the cover of *Rolling Stone,* sporting progressively skimpy and skimpier outfits, signing a multimillion dollar deal with Pepsi. Professionally she could do no wrong. One album after another racked up millions and millions of dollars, and young Britney became a mega-star with power to spare.

Britney remains one of the most successful young blondes of all time. Where she goes from here only she— and her hairdresser—knows for sure.

BLONDE
bon mots

66 *Every night, I have to read a book, so that my
mind will stop thinking about things that I stress about.*

*I always call my cousin because we're so close. We're almost
like sisters, and we're also close because our moms are sisters.*

*I always listen to 'NSYNC's Tearin' Up My Heart.
It reminds me to wear a bra.*

I did not have implants; I just had a growth spurt.

Chocolate for me is just like an orgasm.

*I don't understand the whole dating thing. I know right off the bat if I'm
interested in someone, and I don't want them to waste their money on
me and take me out to eat if I know I'm not interested in that person.*

I don't want people kissing my butt.

*I like meeting all my fans and signing autographs, although
it can all get a bit crazy. Yesterday, for example, a boy just came
over and planted a big kiss on my face! I was like, 'Hello?"*

I don't want to pierce anything. I think it's outdated.
Belly rings and all are, like, old.

I go out with friends, but I don't have time to get in trouble.

I know not everyone will like me, but this is who I am,
so if you don't like it, tough!

I remember I read this harsh review about my show, and
one of my friends told me that this was the exact same stuff
people said about Madonna. And it's like, she didn't care.
Madonna just came out and was herself. I respect that a lot.

I still have a lot to learn—about the business,
about music, and about myself.

My morals are really, you know, strong, and I have major
beliefs about certain things and I think that has helped me,
you know, from being, you know, coming from a really small town.

I wish my hair was thicker, and I wish my feet were prettier.
My toes are really ugly. I wish my ears were smaller.
And my nose could be smaller, too.

The cool thing about being famous is traveling. I have always wanted to
travel overseas, like to Canada and stuff.

I would really, really, really like to be a legend like Madonna.
Madonna knows what to do next, and when she's performing,
the audience is just in awe of her.

Marry Prince William? I'd love that.
Who wouldn't want to be a princess?

Onstage I'm the happiest person in the world.

Just because I look sexy on the cover of Rolling Stone
doesn't mean I'm a naughty girl.

When you're comfortable with someone you love, the
silence is the best.

I want to wait to have sex until I'm married.

I don't really have time to sit down and write. But when I think of a
melody, I call up my answering machine and sing it, so I won't forget it.

The music business has let me touch a lot of people with my talent.

I am a natural blonde and dye my hair brown.

I'm not a little girl anymore. **99**

resources

On Blondes, by Joanna Pitman, Bloomsbury USA, 2003, New York and London.

The Blonde, by Barnaby Conrad III, Chronicle Books, 1999, San Francisco.

www.4reference.com

www.a-ten.com

www.about.com

www.absolutedivas.com

www.absolutenow.com

www.achievement.org

www.actressgallery.com

www.allmovieportal.net

www.amazon.com

www.amiannoying.com

www.amusingquotes.com

www.angelfire.com

www.aol.com

www.ariga.com

www.beautyworlds.com

www.bioterrorhelp.com

www.blondes.net

www.bombshell.com

www.brainyencyclopedia.com

www.brainyquote.com

www.brainyquotes.com

www.britneyspears.com

www.bombshells.com

www.callaway.com

www.cbc.ca

www.cblpolicyinstitute.org

www.celebritystorm.com

www.celebritywonder.com

www.cinema.com

www.cnn.com

www.creativequotations.com

www.cyber-nation.com

www.dailycelebrations.com

www.donkeysmouth.com

www.encyclopedia.com

www.eonline.com

www.famouscreativewomen.com

www.famous-quotations.com

www.feminist.com

www.findarticles.com

www.geocities.com
www.geometry.net
www.handwriting.org
www.heroism.org
www.hollywood.com
www.home2.com
www.hoover.org
www.imdb.com
www.infoplease.com
www.janegoodall.org
www.jaynemansfield.com
www.lkwdpl.org
www.loc.gov
www.margaretthatcher.com
www.msn.com
www.muchmusic.net
www.musicolympics.com
www.msn.com
www.mtv.com
www.netglimpse.com
www.people.com
www.platinum-celebs.com
www.premierespeakers.com
www.quotationspage.com
www.quotationsreference.com
www.quoteworld.org

www.renee-web.com
www.rollingstone.com
www.rockonthenet.com
www.rwitherspooon.com
www.saidwhat.com
www.slogans.net
www.spicyquotes.com
www.sperience.org
www.smh.com
www.thanksforthemusic.com
www.thestreet.com
www.thinkexist.com
www.townsend.com
www.todayinliterature.com
www.toutsurdeneuve.free.fr
www.tripod.com
www.uksociety.org
www.whitehouse.gov
www.who2.com
www.wisdomquotes.com
www.worldofquotes.com
www.wsws.org
www.xplore.com
www.yahoo.com
www.zpub.com

ALPHABETIZED
blonde index

about the author

Writer and editor Paula Munier was born a blonde and has dedicated countless hours and dollars since to staying that way. Towheaded throughout her childhood, by her early teens she was less a golden blonde and more of a dirty blonde. But her fourteenth summer she discovered Sun-In, and presto! Platinum! Her horrified father made her dye her hair back to dirty blonde, but as she told him, "You can change my hair color, but you can't change me!" By sixteen, she'd won the War of the Locks and was the bright yellow blonde she was born to be—and she's never looked back. Thanks to Revlon's streaking kits (1980s), Clairol's Nice & Easy (1990s), and L'Oreal's Feria (2000s), she's as blonde as ever. Forget gray—Ms. Munier is prepared to die a blonde, one way or another.

ALSO FROM FAIR WINDS PRESS

THE MARTINI DIET
by Jennifer "Gin" Sander
ISBN: 1-59233-046-0
$19.00/$12.99/$26.95 CAN
Hardcover; 192 pages
Available wherever books are sold

Spoil yourself thin!
A glass of red wine, a bit of dark chocolate, a petite filet mignon—now that's a diet for the self-indulgent. And why not indulge? Good food and drink is good for you—so say a host of medical studies—all of which you'll find outlined in this deliciously slimming bible for civilized dieters.

With *The Martini Diet*, you'll never need to deprive yourself. You can abandon those awful restrictive diets and punishing workouts at the gym. Have a martini and relax, and let the chic and slender Jennifer "Gin" Sander show you how to lead a happy and healthy life of self-indulgence. You'll learn:

~ Why you should choose Julia Child over Jenny Craig
~ Why French people can eat so much rich food and drink so much wine
  and still be thin and suffer less heart disease than we do
~ Why alcohol, olive oil, chocolate, and salmon are good for you
~ How to kiss the gym goodbye and take up more elegant athletic pursuits
~ How to eat fat and be skinny
~ The three secrets to staying thin forever
~ Fabulous *Martini Diet* recipes

So spoil yourself thin with *The Martini Diet*. Inside you'll find all the ways in which you can indulge yourself and get into shape at the same time. Not only will you live longer, you'll have a heck of a lot more fun.

A longtime fan of self-indulgence, martini-sipping Jennifer (known to her friends as "Gin") is the best-selling author of more than a dozen books, including *Wear More Cashmere* and the best-selling *Christmas Miracles*. The busy mother of two boys, she keeps slim enough to slip into those size-six vintage Chanel suits by drinking gin and eating red meat. A popular public speaker as well, she lives in Northern California.

ALSO FROM FAIR WINDS PRESS

WEAR MORE CASHMERE
by Jennifer "Gin" Sander
ISBN: 1-59233-142-4
$11.95/£7.99/$17.95 CAN
Paperback; 192 pages
Available wherever books are sold

Inner Princess? Yes, your inner princess.

We all long to feel truly special, worthy of being pampered and cared for and fussed over. And Princesses know we deserve it. In this beautifully designed book, you'll find page after page of ideas to make your humdrum everyday life a tiny bit more indulgent. You will learn to adopt the small, stylish gestures that make you look and feel like million dollars. And it won't cost you a queen's ransom either—this book is about spending time (okay, and maybe a bit of money) creating a more glamorous world for yourself. A world fit for your Inner Princess!

With the elegant, cashmere-clad Jennifer "Gin" Sander as your guide, you'll learn how to live like royalty, coddled and cuddled and courted by a cast of thousands. So sit back on your throne (see #25), call upon your princess within, and start reading.

Your Inner Princess will be glad you did.

Wear More Cashmere will teach you 151 ways to
· FEEL SPECIAL by slipping into bed and treating your skin to the smoothness of high-count cotton sheets.
· LOOK SPECIAL by stepping into a pair of mules and adopting that forties glamour girl air.
· BE SPECIAL by growing pale pink orchids in your bathroom, an uncommonly luxurious hobby.